My People Shall Live

The Autobiography of a Revolutionary LEILA KHALED

My People Shall Live

The Autobiography of a Revolutionary

LEILA KHALED

EDITED BY GEORGE HAJJAR 1973 To Bertrand, Bonnie and Sophie and the children of the earth

"It is not enough to hate and believe in the past to make a revolution.

Hatred and belief in the past are sufficient prods for the rebellion phase.

We must love and be future-oriented if we wish to carry out the revolution."

— Ghassan Kanafani, Editor, Al-Hadaf, the organ of the Popular Front for the Liberation of Palestine.

Digitalization & layout by Ole Sandberg, 2008 Foreword by
Lieut.-General Sir John Glubb, KCB, CMG,
DSO, OBE, MC

I SHOULD PERHAPS BEGIN THIS FOREWORD BY EXPLAINING that Miss Leila Khaled did not ask me to write it. I do not know her present whereabouts. Perhaps she does not know that I am writing it. Indeed, in the book itself, she expresses a low opinion of me.

This is a remarkably interesting book for a number of reasons. It is written with extreme simplicity. This is refreshing in a book on Palestine, a subject on which innumerable books have been written. Nearly all of them are prejudiced, if not pure propaganda, and most of them contain half-truths, distortions of the facts, and intentional forms of deception.

Not that Miss Khaled is impartial, but her position is clear. The Israelis have conquered her country by force and driven out her people. She intends to enable them to return.

Throughout the book, she relates simple facts without comment. Her family home in Haifa was seized, the furniture carted away by Jews, who deported her father to Egypt. In the light of this simple narrative, the propaganda seems absurd, which claims that the Palestinians voluntarily abandoned their homes and their possessions to become penniless refugees. The rape of Arab women by Israeli soldiers and the torture of Arab prisoners by the Israeli police are referred to in passing in the same unemotional tone and without comment.

But while her own experiences are narrated factually and simply, her political opinions largely reflect the oversimplified views of the extreme left-wing Palestine parties. The Palestinians have been treated with so much cruelty and injustice that it is not surprising that they should develop a persecution complex. Yet this factor makes it difficult for their sympathizers to assist them, for all their attempts to help are denounced as treachery and deception.

Like other young revolutionaries, Miss Khaled divides the world into good guys and bad guys. The United States comes in for the most severe denunciation as "a nation of monsters and scoundrels."

But perhaps the most obvious moral of the book is that **violence breeds violence**.

- The Nazis subjected the Jews to violence.
- The Jews treated the Palestinians with violence.
- The Palestinians see violence as the only means of recovering their country and their freedom.

At the age of twenty, Leila Khaled wrote, "armed struggle is the way of salvation. As a Palestinian, I had to believe in the gun as an embodiment of my humanity and my determination to liberate myself and my fellow men." Any Palestinians who oppose the use of violence are denounced by her as traitors, fascists, or reactionaries. She relies on the workers and the peasants to rise against all such.

This double objective—**freeing Palestine** and **eliminating all Arab "reactionaries"**—made united action impossible. Indeed, the enemy most bitterly attacked by Leila Khaled and her comrades was Jordan. If the Palestinians had been able to unite to free their country regardless of political ideologies, the result might have been different.

Yet this determined young woman did not call on her comrades to exterminate the Israelis or to drive them into the sea. When victory is won, she says, we will establish a **democratic state in Palestine** with Jews and native Palestinians on equal terms. We will never agree to a solution in which all power is in the hands of one race and the other is reduced to a subordinate status. Her solution is, however, impossible because the basis of Zionism is the desire to have an all-Jewish state and on no account a binational state.

Our sweeping denunciations of hijackers as savage brutes and criminals are somewhat weakened when we read that this famous female hijacker wept when she heard of the assassination of John Kennedy. She emphasizes her determination that her hijackings would not result in loss of human life, especially not in injury to children. And in fact, no one was ever hurt in these enterprises, except her own companion. The object, she explains, was to show the world that the Palestinians were still alive and to be reckoned with.

The author's descriptions of her hijacking exploits are vividly written and most exciting. We do not often have the opportunity to hear an account of such incidents written by the hijacker rather than by the victims.

"He jests at scars, that never felt a wound," says William Shakespeare in Romeo and Juliet.

It is easy for us, who have never been the victims of foreign conquest and are still living in our homes, to denounce with vehemence the crimes of the evicted Palestinians.

**Prefatory Note**

On December 16, 1970, I met Leila Khaled for the first time. It was a brief encounter; I only had the opportunity to ask what she was doing.

"I am a Palestinian Arab soldier," she said proudly. She had read about my radical activities in North America and asked what I was doing. I answered: "I am painting wings of freedom on my shackles!"

We met again on January 4, 1971—I asked if she'd consider writing her memoirs with me. "What memoirs?" she replied, laughing. I insisted that many people would be interested in her experiences. "I'll think about it," she promised.

I saw Leila again on July 23, 1971, and we talked for more than thirty hours over a five-day period. We collected her notes and looked over the published and unpublished material about her. During the following September and October, I wrote this book as told to me by Leila Khaled.

October 30, 1971,

George Hajjar,

Dept. of Integrated Studies,

University of Waterloo, Waterloo, Ontario.

Introduction

The **forced exodus of the Palestinian people** from their ancestral homeland is one of the most dramatic stories of modern times. Yet, after a quarter of a century, that story remains for the most part untold. The picture presented to the outside world is that communicated by the hollow political and military pronouncements of the Arab states or by the Israeli Zionist conquerors and the World Zionist Organisation.

Palestinians have not spoken for themselves; their self-appointed trustees and mediators act without authorization. My generation—the generation of Leila Khaled and the Popular Front—intends to speak for itself with a true Arab revolutionary voice. The echo shall be heard in the coming decades; it is this very voice that the forces of reaction and darkness—Arab, Israeli, and imperialist alike—are hoping to still forever.

The graduates of Auschwitz and the mythical "pioneers" of the third Aliya who founded the Zionist state are responsible for the persecution, dispersion, and continuous alienation of the Palestinian people. As European settlers, they imported with them not only European and American technology but the West's contempt for native populations. Those interlopers and their fabled Sabra offspring dominate the government, the military and labor federation, and every socio-economic institution in Israel.

The sanctimonious attitude of the ruling clique towards their own technological and cultural superiority is further reinforced by a chronic Masada siege mentality that feeds on its own self-induced paranoia. The terror is of an impending holocaust waged by Holy Arab Warriors against poor, besieged Zion, the latter, of course, being a self-helping, self-cultivating, self-determining, peaceful community. This Manichean state of mind has been exploited by the World Zionist Organisation to extort funds from Jews and guilt-ridden liberals the world over.

The WZO, as the loyal servant of imperialism, has been able to deceive the public and win over Western governments because it speaks the language of the West.

More than a half-century has elapsed since the barbaric and systematic obliteration of the Palestinian people began. Nearly a quarter-century has passed since Leila Khaled was evicted from her home in Haifa. Leila was expelled from her homeland in 1948, at the age of four. Her home on Stanton Street in Haifa is now occupied by European Zionists who claimed to have a "higher right" than she did.

Leila became a "refugee" child, one of the hundreds of thousands of Palestinians forced out of their country to make room for the victims of European inhumanity. Leila was among the more fortunate Palestinians; her family lived in one room rather than in a tent in a refugee camp. Yet she knows by personal experience what it means to be a refugee. She is now a full-time revolutionary, discovering the true meaning of being a Palestinian in its original Canaan definition: a heroic fighter, a warlike person, a selfless fellow.

To Leila, history has determined her vocation, and destiny has decreed her role. To the Palestinian and Arab people, Leila is the symbol of liberated womanhood, the devoted patriot who, with the Popular Front, will end tyranny and exploitation in the Arab homeland. To the friends of revolution everywhere, Leila is hope restored, humanity rediscovered, self-respect regained.

This book is not a historic document, nor is it an academic analysis of the highly complicated Arab-Zionist-imperialist civil war of the past quarter-century. It is rather the personal portrait of a Palestinian revolutionary who lived through the period as a child of revolution and as a participant-observer. Revolutionaries and lovers have yet to write of the struggle. Leila Khaled is a revolutionary and a humanist. This is her story and the story of her people and their fight for freedom.

Leila generously gave her time and talent to the task of reconstructing her life as a revolutionary. Thanks also must go to her comrades for their help in creating this book.

PART ONE: The Badge of Infamy - Deprivation and Discovery

---

## The Staircase

Come forward, poor of the earth, and cover this time with tatters and tears. Cover it with the body that seeks its warmth, the city: arcs of madness. I thought Revolution should give birth to its children, so I buried millions of songs and came.

Adonis (Quoted in Mona Saudi's *In Time of War! Children Testify*, p. 168)

I COME FROM THE CITY OF HAIFA, BUT I REMEMBER LITTLE of my birthplace.

I can see the area where I played as a small child, but of our house, I only remember the staircase. I was taken away when I was four, not to see Haifa again for many years. Finally, I saw my city twenty-one years later, on August 29, 1969, when Comrade Salim Issawi and I expropriated an imperialist plane and returned to Palestine to pay homage to our occupied country and to show that we had not abandoned our homeland. Ironically, the Israeli enemy, powerless, escorted us with his French and American planes.

What I knew about Haifa had come from my parents and friends and from books. Now I saw Haifa from the air and formed my own cherished image of my home. Haifa is caressed by the sea, hugged by the mountain, inspired by the open plain. Haifa is a safe anchor for the wayfarer, a beach in the sun. Yet, I, as a citizen of Haifa, am not allowed to bask in its sun, breathe its clear air, live there with my people. European Zionists and their followers are living in Palestine by right of arms, and they have expelled us from our homeland. They live where we should be living while we float about, exiled. They live in my city because they are Jews and they have power. My people and I live outside because we are Palestinian Arabs without power. But we, the graduates of the desert inns, we shall have power, and we shall recover Palestine and make it a human paradise for Arabs and Jews and lovers of freedom.

I love Haifa, as does my family and all Palestinians. At the outset, my love for Haifa was sentimental, a child's love for a dreamland. As I grew older and began to read and think for myself, I discovered that I have historic roots, that my people have a history of struggle, and that my nation is the equal, if not the superior, of other nations. Above all, I learned that my class, the working people, the unemployed, the refugees, and the oppressed everywhere could liberate mankind from the shackles of superstition and backwardness. I had to forget what the colonial school system had endeavored to instill in me—that I had no history; that there was no Palestinian people, no Arab nation. In my search for freedom, I discovered some of our legendary heroes and the golden age of Arabism and realized how "historians" have skillfully belittled our achievements and consigned us to oblivion.

I knew that I had a role to play: I realized that my historic mission was as a warrior in the inevitable battle between oppressors and oppressed, exploiters and exploited. I decided to become a revolutionary in order to liberate my people and myself.

I was greatly inspired by a Palestinian revolutionary of the 1930s: Izz Edeen Kassam, a man who embodied the spirit of resistance and who organized the first working-class and peasant revolution in the Arab homeland. He had been organizing his Underground for several years. In 1935, seeing the continuing betrayal of his people, he launched an armed struggle which he intended to be the beginning of a people's war of liberation against the enemies: British imperialism, Zionism, and Arab backwardness. The revolutionaries were workers, peasants, students, and other progressive groups. The revolt was a revolt of the oppressed, and it was suppressed by the British with the aid of the Zionists and Arab reactionaries. Palestine was lost to Zionism between 1936 and 1939, not between 1946 and 1948 as historians would have us believe. In 1936, a peasant uprising engulfed the entire country in a general strike that lasted from April to October. Its goal was to ensure Palestinian Arab identity by the establishment of a democratic state, the expulsion of the British, and the cessation of Zionist innmigration to Palestine. The only result was that the British set up one of their time-honored imperial devices: the Royal Commission, which in 1937 recommended the partition of Palestine. The Defence Party of Palestine—a front organization of King Abdullah and the British—agreed to the proposal. The revolutionary struggle intensified, but resistance was finally crushed by a traitorous Palestinian leadership and its "peace regiments"; by Arab government trusteeship and its "mediation"; and finally by British-Zionist military collaboration. Kassam was martyred. His martyrdom precipitated a political cataclysm, but his revolution was finally buried by his enemies; his memory was blotted out by his detractors. The Popular Front for the Liberation of Palestine begins where Kassam left off: his generation started the revolution; my generation intends to finish it.

I learned the history of the upheaval of the 1936 revolution largely from books, but I know the history of my people since 1948 from the bitterness of my own experience. I left Haifa four days after my fourth birthday, on April 13, 1948. My birthday was not celebrated because April 9 was a day of national mourning in Palestine. I am now twenty-nine years old, and I have not celebrated a single birthday since, and will not do so until I return to Haifa. I did not leave Haifa of my own free wish. The decision was not made by my family but by a people who should have known better—a persecuted and hunted race who in turn became my persecutors and hunters of my brethren.

My family had cordial relations with our Jewish neighbors. We lived on Stanton Street, which wasn't far from the Jewish quarter, Hadar, the fashionable Fifth Avenue of Haifa. I knew Jewish children; Tamara, one of my best friends, was Jewish, but I knew that there was no distinction between us. I was conscious of being neither Arab nor Jew. The turning point in my relationship with Tamara came on November 29, 1947, when the UN partitioned Palestine between Tamara and me. Tamara was awarded 56 percent of my land. (Her own people claimed only eight percent ownership of the whole land of Palestine, according to their own statistics.) I was expected to accede to this demand and congratulate Tamara's people. I was expected to deny my humanity, acknowledge the moral legitimacy of the Zionist claims, and accept the status of being homeless in my own home, a refugee in my own land. World Zionism, American imperialism, and all their allies sentenced me to a life of exile for being an Arab. Then they expected us to honor their "decision" and abide by it. Because, if we bided by that "decision," Zionist claims would be satisfied, their territorial expansion would end, and their Aliyahs' immigrations would cease.

The UN "decision" to partition Palestine prompted a general strike that lasted for three days. The strike was totally ineffective. The Arab National Movement was exhausted; it was a mere ghost, a disorganized, emotional mob. The traditional institutions disintegrated; the newer confederations of workers and peasants weren't sufficiently developed to take up the cause of national liberation. We were foredoomed. Sporadic violence broke out: Arabs killed Jews, Jews killed Arabs. But Jewish violence was organized and disciplined. They were thoroughly mobilized and they knew what they were fighting for. Arab violence was ill-planned, random activity carried on by individuals. The Zionists had camaraderie as well as gunpowder; they had well-organized armed forces and they excelled in psychological warfare. Their leaders were at the head of their columns; ours were securely ensconced in Mount Lebanon or Cairo. The Zionists were thus able to snatch Haifa out from under us, particularly after Sir John Glubb Pasha, the commander of the Arab Legion of Jordan, ordered his Haifa regiment to withdraw in agreement with British plans to evacuate Haifa and ensure Jewish victory.

With careful coordination and brilliant military strategy, the Zionists thought they could attain their goal with a minimum of effort and loss of life. They did. Most of the 80,000 Arab inhabitants of Haifa left without battling to the death for their city. They departed in an atmosphere of terrorism. This exodus started on April 9, my birthday, the day the Zionists massacred in cold blood the people of Deir Yassin—a crime which the Zionists cruelly but cleverly magnified to frighten the remaining population into submissive departure. Haifa was electrified by the murder of 254 people and the wounding of hundreds more. The people of Haifa feared that they were on the eve of a much greater massacre. Terror and panic prevailed.

Two days later the violence touched me: I saw death for the first time. I do remember being terrified, but I do not remember whether the dead person was Arab or Jew. I only remember hearing bombs exploding and seeing the blood spurting from the dying man's stomach. I hid under the staircase and stared at the corpse in the street outside. I trembled and wondered whether this would be the fate of my father.

The spread of death and terror, and fear for our future, impelled my family and most other Arabs to leave. The eight of us and my mother left for Sour on April 13, 1948. My instinctive reaction was that I must remain at home. Nobody explained to me why we were leaving, and I didn't understand.

Mother packed the children into the little rented car with a few of our personal belongings and was ready to set off until she counted the children and found that one was missing. All knew instantly that I was the one. Two of my sisters found me hiding behind the date box and hauled me out like a sack of potatoes. Nawal screamed, "The Jews will kill you if you don't come!" as she pulled me by the hair. I was infuriated and still couldn't understand why we were going to Sour. My father bade us farewell, gave me a tearful kiss, and remained behind. I remember the figure of despair growing smaller in the distance. I also remember that this was the last time I saw the staircase of our house.

I didn't see my father again for several months.

And when he came to Sour, he was a broken man. Apparently, my father had had no intention of leaving; he intended to remain no matter who controlled Haifa. However, our home and his business were seized on April 22, immediately after the fall of Haifa. He had to watch Zionists moving into our home. He saw our furniture carted off.

Then he, himself, was deported to Egypt. My father managed to reach Sour by the late summer of 1948. He arrived penniless after working hard for three decades as a storekeeper. Never allowed to become a Lebanese citizen, my father truly felt the meaning of rejection. He was thrown out of his country and then denied citizenship in a neighboring Arab country. He remained exiled in Lebanon until his death in 1966. For eighteen long years, he lived in Lebanon dreaming of returning to Haifa. I, as his daughter, am attempting to realize that dream. I shall not fail my father and my nation. If I am unable to return and live in freedom in Palestine, my children will return.

Historians and the pliable Western media try to tell us that the people of Haifa left their city while the Jewish mayor called for co-existence and co-operation. Even if we presume the mayor's call to have been genuine, would that have stopped the bloodshed and the systematic expulsion of my people? Would that have suddenly made the Zionists change their program of conquest and subjugation of the Arabs? If the mayor had been sincere, why didn't he command his Zionist hordes to cease firing? Why didn't he stop the murder of my brothers and the rape of my sisters? If the Zionists desired co-existence, why did they and the "innocent" British prepare hundreds of little boats to transport the people of Haifa to Sour, Saida, and Acre? Zionist deeds were more eloquent than their words. The Zionists wanted us out of Haifa and Palestine, and they succeeded in forcing us to leave while making the world believe we left voluntarily. We did not leave voluntarily, and if we did, what law or morality gave the Zionists the right to occupy our homes and take our possessions? That is the question which the realistic historian must answer and the fact that every self-respecting Jew must live with.

It is also reported that the Palestinian Arabs hoped to return to their homes after the "invading" Arab armies had reoccupied Haifa, driven the Jews into the sea, and restored their rights. As to "invading" Arab armies, the so-called seven Arab states dispatched some twenty thousand-odd troops under the most adverse conditions. They were neither well-trained nor equipped with modern weapons. They faced an enemy with over 60,000 committed and trained troops. The Arabs had no central command and no morale to speak of. If any heroic deeds were achieved, they were the deeds of individuals, not armies. The Arab armies were merely the sacrificial lamb of a dying social order that sent a mob of soldiers to face a modern enemy, thinking it could win an easy victory and take a new lease on life. The Arab "invasion," as it turned out, merely gave the Zionists a pretext to add a substantial proportion of the UN-created Arab Palestine to the Jewish share and enabled King Abdullah and his Palestinian cohorts to obliterate the country of Palestine by annexing the remainder of Palestine to Jordan. Moreover, the Arab "intervention" gave the Israelis a feeling of invincibility.

I vividly remember my mother saying to me, shortly after our arrival in Lebanon, that I must not pick oranges from the grove nearby. I was puzzled and insisted on knowing why. My poor mother, with tears streaming from her eyes, explained: "Darling, the fruit is not ours; you are no longer in Haifa; you are in another country." Before she rushed into the house to wipe her tears and hide her shame, she looked at me with motherly firmness, saying: "Henceforth you are forbidden to eat oranges that are not ours." With child-like acceptance, I nodded my head, but her words still echo.

For the first time, I began to question the injustice of our exile. As a child of four, I found myself burdened by the adult problems of life and death, right and wrong. I, as a dreamer, living on the bare subsistence provided by a UN blue ration card, in a crowded room on a side street in Sour, stand as a witness to Zionist inhumanity. I charge the world for its acquiescence in my destruction.

My family and I sank into a mood of quiet despair and settled into a routine of sordid living. Of the summer of 1948, I recall nothing besides accompanying my older sisters Nawal, Zakiah, and Rahaab to the United Nations

Relief and Works Agency (UNRWA) provision bureau to collect our miserable rations. My sisters were humiliated; my mother was angry. While we lived on international charity, the Zionists enjoyed the fruits of our labor in Palestine. Western friends tell me that the Zionists claim that when they "pioneered" Palestine, there were no people there, that there were only malarial swamps and arid deserts which they turned into green plains and rolling valleys. Friends also tell me that the Zionists want peace and that we, the Arab marauders, continuously infiltrate into Palestine to burn, murder, and steal. In the autumn of 1948, I was placed in the Sheikah kindergarten to keep me out of mischief.

I enjoyed the company of the other children. I was quite boyish and aggressive; I played and fought with the boys. Our teacher, Zeinah, was an energetic little old lady who loved children and dedicated her life to them. She truly cared for us and taught us to care for our fellow men. She was an upright and strong person and sought to pass on her values to us, but the children didn't seem to appreciate her sermons.

We had no program of study at school. It was merely a babysitting affair, but Zeinah was a devoted Muslim matron who thought that teaching us the Holy Koran was a noble mission.

Without teaching us the alphabet or giving us any other kind of instruction, she asked us, children between the ages of five and six, to commit substantial portions of the Koran to memory, and we did. Graduation from Sheikah was no easy task. Each prospective graduate had to recite sections of the Koran in public—almost like a doctoral defense for children. I delighted in my own word-perfect performance, particularly when I was reciting the story of Joseph and how he fled to Egypt with the child Jesus to escape death at the hands of Herod, but was later banished at the behest of the Pharisees, the higher Jewish clergy, the Zionist prototypes. The teacher and the children were overjoyed. I was ecstatic. As I finished the last verse, a child ran from the schoolhouse carrying the news to my mother and demanding alHilweinah, a worthwhile reward. My poor mother could only afford to give her a few sweets. When I arrived home, cheerfully announcing my graduation, my mother also gave me some sweets and a big kiss. I had expected a gift and a big celebration, but nothing happened. I cried my eyes out, not realizing that my mother was unable to buy me a dress, a doll, or even a pair of socks.

My Uncle Kahmoud, who did have money, had heard the news. He asked me whether it was true.

I said, "Yes." He gave me a little test and was very impressed. He couldn't believe that a child of six could have memorized whole portions of the Koran. To show his appreciation, he gave me one whole Lebanese pound (the equivalent of 25 pence). This was the first pound I had ever earned. I jumped with joy, gave him a great big hug, and ran home to announce the big victory to my mother and to emphasize her niggardliness. Mother smiled approvingly as I displayed the pound and boasted about the generosity of my uncle, her brother. But I had no idea of what to do with my prize, so I gave it to my mother. She returned to me twenty-five piastres, saying, "This is yours, Leila, do as you wish with it." A few days later, I bought a gift for my teacher and sweets for the children with my treasure. In the autumn of 1950, I was enrolled in grade one at the Union of Evangelical Churches' School for the Palestinians, but only after a struggle. That summer, I had learned to read on my own by attentively listening to my sisters and picturing the passages of the Koran in my mind. Since I was Zakiah's constant companion, I knew what she knew and learned what she learned. She was going into the fourth grade, and I decided I wanted to be in the same grade, especially after discovering that the two pre-elementary grades plus the first two grades were going to be housed in a tent on the grounds of the schoolhouse.

But the teacher placed me in the first preelementary grade and proceeded as if nothing was wrong.

I was shocked and objected strenuously. I shouted out that I ought to be placed in grade four. Everyone laughed.

"Examine me and you will see," I demanded. I was able to read fourth-grade level Arabic without making a mistake. Then she examined me in mathematics, and I knew enough to pass. English was my downfall. I knew the alphabet and a few words that my sisters used around the house. I was able to recognize the English alphabet as she wrote it on the blackboard, but I made a disastrous mistake when I read the letter "O" in English as "five" in Arabic, which in fact took the same form. The teacher burst out laughing. "You see, I knew you didn't know enough to be even in grade two, never mind grade four. But since you're such a bright little girl, you won't have to spend two years in pre-elementary school. I will place you in grade one." I made my point and achieved a real academic victory, but I also felt a momentary letdown because I still had to remain in the tent outside the schoolhouse. Henceforth, I was no longer a child learning songs and games, but a serious pupil learning Arabic, math, and English. Also, as a student in grade one, I earned the right to my own slate with a sponge and lead chalk. Mother made me a cloth school bag from a piece of one of her old dresses. I was delighted that I had so much!

In grades one and two, I enjoyed school and settled down to a "normal" existence in exile. There was only one significant incident during these years in my life, which had to do with demonstrations commemorating the loss of Palestine. Although I was passionately aware of the Palestinian tragedy, for some reason or other, I thought the demonstration on May 15, 1951, was a mere interference with my schoolwork. The school was closed for the occasion, but I did not participate. I asked Mother what the demonstrations meant. Realizing that I was the only child of walking age who had remained at home, she replied angrily, "As a Palestinian girl, you should have joined your sisters to protest against the Zionist occupation of Palestine." I agreed that the demonstration was desirable but insisted that schoolwork was more important.

Mother was surprised by my treasonous talk and lectured me on the three historic days of betrayal that every Palestinian should remember: the Balfour Declaration of November 2, 1917; the partition of Palestine, November 29, 1947; and the proclamation of the state of Israel, May 15, 1948. Ever since, these dates have become a vital and integral part of my life.

1952 was a turning point in my life. I was only eight years old, but the onrush of events and the background of my world of exile forced me to be politically aware. My brother first drew me into politics. I recall the first political debate between brother Mohammad and my father. Mohammad, who was 17, was enthusiastically relating to the family how a group of young Egyptian army officers overthrew the corrupt King Farouk of Egypt. Father was opposed to the revolt and insisted that the officers were a group of military upstarts who knew nothing about politics and overthrew a king who had fought for the defense of Palestine in 1948. Mohammad was furious. He reminded father that the King was a British political stooge who lost the war in Palestine and did nothing for four years to help recover Palestine. Moreover, Mohammad continued, "The King and his retinue were decadent to the bones and they squandered the wealth of Egypt on themselves rather than on the people." The family was cheering for Mohammad as he proved that he was better informed than father. Mohammad had collected the documentary evidence from Rose EI-Yousef – an Egyptian journal – and pasted it on the wall of the boys' room. He read it all to father, who acquiesced and proudly congratulated his eldest son on being so well informed and committed to the revolution.

Mohammad became our political commentator, and all of us, especially the girls, learned enormously from him. Furthermore, being at the American University of Beirut on a scholarship added to his prestige and put him in close association with the fledgling Arab Youth Movement, which provided him with a wealth of information and organizational skill.

In the autumn of 1952, I enrolled at the same "exclusive" Palestinian school set up by the churches.

This was the year of discovery and commitment. In the next three or four years, my political and social ideas were formed, and my political ties were made. A series of unrelated incidents set the stage for my politicization: a violent storm; a harsh cold; a collection for a refugee girl. The pleasant summer of 1952 turned into a violent winter in early December. A storm struck and blew over our school tent, which held over seventy children. A few were injured; the rest of us had the daylights scared out of us. In the midst of pouring icy rain, tears, and mud, I stood silently crying as the children screamed and ran for cover. It was a symbol of our ruined Arab homeland. Local protests and heartrending stories followed, but to no avail. Western Christian charity had its limits.

The tent was re-erected; there was no alternative. At this point, the tent had little or no meaning to me. It was not long after this incident that it began to dawn on me that tens of thousands of people permanently lived in tents, not just for games or schooling. In early 1953, a bitter cold spell set in in Sour; beautiful white snow covered the mountains of Lebanon and the mountains of Galilee. Slush and ice covered the whole town. I caught a bad cold, but we had no medicine, and I had to keep on going to school in my worn-out sandals. One windy February day, I struggled home through nearly two feet of snow. I was freezing to death. I entered the house crying pitifully.

I shouted, "I can't take any more! I need a pair of socks and a pair of shoes. Sandals without socks are for the summer, not for the winters of Lebanon."

Mother looked at me sadly. "Darling, don't you think I know that?"

"If you did," I screamed, "you'd buy me a pair of shoes and socks."

Angrily, she answered, "You should be thankful you have a pair of sandals to wear and a house to come to. Other children have neither sandals nor homes. They don't even have enough to eat. Do you understand, Leila? Do you?"

"No, I don't," I replied angrily. But I enquired further. "Why don't they have sandals, homes, and bread? Why don't they have them?"

Mother replied quietly: "They have no money because their parents are like us; they lost their homes in Palestine, and there is no work available in Lebanon. You see, Leila, those Palestinians who had no relatives elsewhere in the Arab world had no place to go but the open desert or the slums of Arab towns and somehow survive until UNRWA was organized. Imagine where we might have landed had we not had relatives in Sour, and I had not had a few bracelets from the old days which I could sell to buy you food for the first few months. Where would we have gone? Where would we be now? I wonder if you would have survived to this day. What might have happened to you and your sisters and brothers had I been killed or taken away by the Zionists when we were on our way from Haifa to Sour? Don't you know that the Zionists slaughtered our people, and those who escaped them died of thirst or starvation? I could tell you a million tales of woe, but I want you to know only this: you are an alien here in Lebanon, and your homeland is under foreign occupation. We fought and fought valiantly to save the land; we lost and were driven out. You, Leila, and your brothers and sisters must never forget Palestine, and you must do your utmost to recover her."

I imagined I was listening to a sad story that had happened somewhere else to someone else. I was affected deeply, but I didn't feel that I was part of the story.

The truth finally hit me in the spring of 1953 when I was nine. I was competitive and regarded myself as the brightest child of not only my family but of my class. My self-assurance was undermined by Samirah, a little girl from the camps—the scum of the earth, so I thought. I was terribly upset when I learned that she stood first in the class, way ahead of me. I despised her; my jealousy overwhelmed me. I think I even hit her, and I certainly insulted her. Once we even fought in the classroom.

When the teacher discovered us locked in a hair-pulling match, she promptly separated us, surprised to see her two smartest pupils fighting. Outside, the fighting resumed; I was the aggressor once again. The teacher took me inside for a little talk; it was a talk I shall never forget. She explained to me that poor peasant children were just as bright as my family and friends.

"Besides," she added, "they are the true children of Palestine because they live on the land and cultivate and harvest it. Virtue is a part of the people of the land, and the simple folk are the backbone of all societies. Those peasants," she continued, "did not leave Palestine willingly like the rich people who now live in villas in Cairo and Beirut. They were forced out to make room for the Zionist intruders. Leila, those are the people of

Palestine. You must learn to love them, be part of them, serve them."

The lesson taught, she called Samirah back into the room and told her to shake hands with me and to take me to her tent-home to show me how she lived and how her parents and hundreds of thousands of Palestinians lived. Samirah did. After a tour of the camp, I realized that I was living in luxury. I knew how fortunate I was and how despicable and arrogant the rich people must be.

I suddenly became aware of class differences in that upsetting spring for me. As I grew older, I acquired the necessary intellectual and moral ideology to understand what I had felt in that camp, why class society must be abolished and socialism established in its place. But Samirah, my classmate and class sister, and

Amirah, my teacher and working-class advocate, taught me that first lesson of true freedom and true humanity. They taught me more in a few hours than a thousand books could have done in a hundred years.

In that camp, I saw misery, hunger, and humiliation. I saw the maimed, the diseased, the broken-hearted. I saw barefooted children with swollen stomachs, fathers with heads bowed, pale mothers with sickly babies, grandparents in despair. I saw the meaning of poverty and hunger and felt the despair of deprivation to my bones.

I did not shy away at the sight of filthy tents, and I was not deterred by the sight of death. I toured the whole camp and tried to feel how the people felt. I returned home intoxicated by the wine of reality. I was crucified and redeemed at the same time. Ever since, I have loved the poor and marched with them to overthrow our mutual oppressors. Over 700,000 Palestinians still live in these refugee camps. Some of them do menial work in nearby towns; most of them rot in idleness. They live on meager UN doles and have no hope of salvation without an Arab Palestinian revolution.

My faith in myself and my fellow students was greatly strengthened in the spring of 1953. On Bayram's Eve, the Easter of Islam, most of the children were ready for a week's vacation. Most were talking about dolls, dresses, and the other gifts they expected to receive.

A sad little girl in ragged clothes was sitting nearby all by herself. I didn't know her well, and I didn't ask her why she was so lonely and unhappy. Nabil, our teacher, was aware of her plight. After our break, he told us that it would soon be Easter and that all of us, with the exception of one little girl, would be receiving gifts.

He said, "It would be unmoslem not to share our riches with the poor, and certainly unArab not to be generous." I was excited—maybe the time had come to storm UNRWA's offices or government house in Sour.

But Nabil had no such drastic measures in mind. "One of you will not have a happy Easter unless she has a new dress for the occasion. I cannot afford to buy her a dress alone. Here, I am contributing twenty-five piastres, and if each one of you contributes two to five piastres, we could buy Hassnah a dress."

The children looked at each other, puzzled by the request. I was not. I knew what it meant to be poor, having just visited the primitive camps.

I stood up and announced, "Here is my entire weekly allowance of five piastres." Most of the children followed suit, and we bought Hassnah a dress in the midst of joyous tears. I decided not to wear my own new dress that year because thousands of Palestinian children had none.

I loved my teacher Nabil, adored his physical prowess and moral integrity. He, in turn, coddled me and treated me like a little sister. On the fifth anniversary of the creation of Israel, May 15, 1953, he and I marched at the head of the parade.

With clenched fists, we shouted, "Long live Arab."

"Palestine, Palestine is ours, we shall return!" Thousands of people, old and young, assembled in the town square to hear Nabil swear allegiance to the flag on behalf of all Palestinians. He spoke persuasively, "Our parents lost Palestine, but our succeeding generations have an obligation to liberate our homeland." As he concluded his speech, he asked the crowd to look southward and to pledge before themselves and their fellow men to return to fight for Palestine.

I had received the sacrament of revolution. I also learned a lesson from my cat, Sarah. She was black like me, and we were constant companions. I read my lessons to her; I took her for walks to the sea. I made clothes for her, bathed her, and brushed her like an infant. Sarah was my child. When she had her first litter of kittens, I acted as midwife. I was devoted to the kittens. When one died, I gave him a Muslim burial and visited his grave daily.

Then one day, I discovered a great big chicken eating the flowers off my kitten's grave. I caught him and, in my childish fury, wrung his neck. The incident caused an uproar around the house; finally, the neighbor was dutifully told that her chicken had violated my rights of property. My mother insisted that I dispose of the kittens. After some searching, I found good homes for them.

Then nature took its course, and my cat became pregnant again. My mother was determined not to turn our home into a maternity hospital again, so she seized the cat, put her in a sack, and told my uncle to take her as far away as possible. I cried and pleaded with her, but she was unyielding. Uncle carried out the mission.

I was catless for nearly one year. In the spring of 1954, I was ten years old. On a bright Sunday morning on my way home from school, I saw my cat, Sarah, striding majestically on the top of the arch of a dilapidated building. I was overcome and rushed towards her, not completely certain that it was Sarah. It was indeed my cat, and I welcomed her with open arms. The whole family was overjoyed and regarded her return as miraculous.

On Monday morning, the teacher asked us to write an essay on something very important that had happened in our own lives. I was pleased to have the chance to write on the return of my "dove to the ark." I wrote about the story of the flood, comparing it to the Zionist flooding of Palestine and portraying my cat as the "dove of peace" that foretold of the ebbing of the tide. I felt that if my cat could find her way back to me after one year, I ought to be able to find my way back to a liberated Palestine.

My teacher, also a Palestinian, thought the sentiment was noble and elevating and tried to instill in me a more scientific approach to the homeland. But to a child of ten, the homeland was a dream to excite the imagination, not an attainable goal.

To extinguish the flame of revolution, "safeguard" Arab black gold, and maintain United States strategic interests, America—the creator, protector, and supplier of weapons to Israel; the father, godfather, and high priest of Zionism—set out in the early 1950s to create an extension to NATO and place our world in its orbit. John Foster Dulles, the US Secretary of State, visited the Middle East in March 1953.

His country was in the grip of virulent McCarthyism, and Dulles, as an ardent anti-communist, came to "save" us from the "Communist menace" and turn us into docile "democratic" citizens of the "free world." He sought to form a regional alliance tied to NATO and, at the same time, find a final settlement to the so-called Arab-Israeli conflict, which would ensure the continued supremacy of Western imperialism and its oil cartels in the area.

The answer of my generation to Dulles's attempts was a loud "No"; all the free groups worked together to frustrate his plans. It was rather fitting that opposition should commence at the American University of Beirut. But neither Dulles nor his local supporters were aware of the depth of nationalist feelings that gripped the country. Nationalist students led the struggle for liberty under the vanguard of the Arab Youth Movement. They weren't frightened of death and were not scared off by the armed soldiers who tried to keep them at bay and protect Dulles. Young nationalist revolutionaries broke through the army ranks and almost managed to slay the dragon of capitalism.

Hell broke loose as the resurgent crowds moved towards their target. The army, gendarmerie, and secret police moved in. Dozens of students were seized while hundreds of others were clubbed or crushed by mounted horsemen. My brother Mohammad participated in the demonstration and returned to tell the eager family about it.

Though the country was profoundly shocked by the brutality of its own soldiers, it took another year of nationalist agitation, and finally the murder of Hassan Abu Ismael, the American University of Beirut student leader, for the country to wake up and disentangle itself from the web of the proposed American alliance system—the Baghdad Pact.

The murder of Hassan was particularly terrible because it took place in front of the AUB, and the AUB administration refused to lodge a formal protest against the assassination of one of its students. Suddenly, people began to understand the meaning of Western democratic institutions and their political intentions towards the Middle East.

But the unfolding drama of the fifties did not reach its denouement until the Suez War of 1956. During this conflict, Britain and France, in concert with Israel, invaded Egypt seeking to overthrow Nasser and impose a Ben Gurion kind of peace on the Arab people.

The declaration of May 25, 1950, in which the three great powers—Britain, France, and the USA—had guaranteed the territorial integrity and sovereign independence of the Middle Eastern states and pledged to come to the aid of an aggrieved party, was trampled upon by two of its signatories, Britain and France, and allowed to lapse by America when it was no longer of value to Zionism.

The West failed to coerce the entire Arab world into a subservient alliance system under the wing of America. On the contrary, it forced a polarization in which Nasser's Cairo became the focal point of nationalist awakening and Nuri's Baghdad the center of counter-revolution and the capital of the "northern tier" advocates.

All in all, Dulles and Ike, Eden and Macmillan, Ben Gurion and Moshe Dayan were not a totally unmitigated evil; they gave us a rude awakening for which we owe them a debt of gratitude. They forced us to re-examine the foundations of our society. No longer did the Arabs have to undergo long periods of self-delusion to distinguish friend from foe and to uncover the enemy within and without.

# 2 Education and Revolution

Man is born free and everywhere he is in chains.
*Rousseau*

AS A MEMBER OF THE ARAB NATIONALIST MOVEMENT, I was trained to be conscious of the past, present, and future. Underdeveloped people and societies typically lack an awareness of the present and the future, but such consciousness is imperative if we are to be masters of our own lives and environment. We cannot overcome the past and its crippling ideologies unless we gain a free consciousness.

Underdeveloped people live by fate; they look with nostalgia to a "golden past." My people and I suffer from these debilities, but we are also living in the ongoing process of history and are trying to determine our future rather than bind ourselves to a dead past. The value of the conquest of Palestine by imperialism and Zionism is that it forced some of us to re-examine the foundation of our society on our own. We discovered that our society was rotten, traditional, and unprogressive. Our defeat was indeed our salvation, our means of regeneration and renewal. Now the issue is not restoration, but the construction of a new socialist republic encompassing the entire Arab world.

We must either accept or decline the challenge. If we accept, we must head to the mountains, to the peasants' huts, to the city slums. If we decline, we could lead a life of "happy" servitude under the yoke of Zionism and imperialism and compare our economic well-being today with that of last year or the year before Dayan "liberated" us. Moreover, we could console ourselves by saying, "We now have peace and quiet," and we have more "democracy" under Moshe Dayan and his bulldozers than under Hussein and his Bedouin regiments.

By 1955, I was becoming conscious of present problems and future plans. In that spring, I obtained my elementary school certificate and made plans to go on to secondary school. I was eleven years old, and Israel was seven. We went through the same perennial ritual of denouncing Zionism, imperialism, and Arab reactionaries on the seventh anniversary of our exile and doing nothing about it.

Meanwhile, Israel had used those seven years to consolidate her internal front and "integrate" her Afro-Asian population, the Sephardim Jews. "Peace" overtures were made by Moshe Sharrett in 1954, but his government was toppled by the Israeli hawks under the redoubtable leadership of Ben Gurion.

However, before Sharrett's overthrow, the Israeli government was implicated in one of the most insidious plots in the history of diplomacy. The scheme, known as the **Lavon affair**, entailed the blowing up of the US and British embassies and other Western strategic interests in

Egypt to prove the instability of the Egyptian regime and "persuade" Israel's protectors to remain ensconced at Suez and not to withdraw from the Sudan. The Israelis, of course, had hoped to make the crime appear the work of the Egyptians. Unhappily for them, they were caught red-handed and exposed.

The Lavon affair rocked Israeli politics for the next decade. Israeli expansionism began in earnest with:

- The gradual annexation of demilitarized zones set up under the truce agreements of Rhodes (1949)
- The continued expulsion of Arabs from Israel
- The suppression of the remaining Arab minority in Israel

More important was the start of the policy of massive reprisals. This was launched on October 15, 1953, with an attack on the village of Kibya and culminated on February 28, 1955, when Israel invaded the Gaza Strip, demolished Egyptian fortifications, and killed and wounded over one hundred and fifty people. The attack did not have its intended effect. Nasser did not withdraw; instead, he encompassed the entire Arab world.

By the autumn of 1955, he concluded the famous arms deal with Czechoslovakia, thereby breaking the Western monopoly as the sole armament supplier to the Mid-East states and began to move towards pan-Arabism.

Everything crystallized in the early autumn of 1955 because Allen Dulles, the head of the CIA and brother of John Foster Dulles, flew to Cairo in September and tried to persuade President Nasser not to go through with the Czech arms deal. This high-handed gesture, denounced by Arab nationalists, was only the first in a series of attempts on the part of the American imperialists to undermine Nasser.

Hardly any schoolchild that year escaped learning about these events. I anxiously absorbed details and mastered most of the anti-Western arguments.

My family's economic condition improved, and the atmosphere around the house relaxed. We now had a three-room apartment, and hunger was no longer a threat. Two of my sisters were working, and my mother had made some wise investments.

We all felt that the Arabs were taking some overdue first steps towards recovering Palestine, and we were still wholeheartedly behind the nationalist movement.

1956 was the year of years in modern Arab history. The Nasserite regime, aided by external and internal pressures, had managed to extract an evacuation agreement from the British in 1954, and by June 1956, withdrawal was completed. Dulles and Eden then decided to topple Nasser because he was moving in a neutralist direction instead of toeing the Western line. They exerted economic pressures, but he did not yield.

Nasser was beginning to sense his potential power and the desire of the Arab masses for a strong, charismatic leader. Eden and Dulles, for their part, were unable to grasp the profound changes that were taking place. They thought that if they couldn't overthrow Nasser, they could humiliate him and make waves by withdrawing the promised $70 million loan for the Aswan High Dam project.

Nasser responded by nationalizing the Suez Canal on July 26, 1956. The Arab giant had suddenly awakened and roared with fury at the West. Mass adulation for Nasser became an Arab phenomenon; Nasserism became a worldwide doctrine. The West was stunned when Arab pilots soon proved that they could operate the Canal just as, if not more, competently than their Western counterparts.

The world stopped and listened. Diplomats from the Third World made pilgrimages to Cairo to declare their solidarity with the Arabs. When Robert Menzies, the Prime Minister of Australia, journeyed to Cairo carrying the ultimatum of the Canal Users' Association, Nasser gave Menzies an emphatic no and sent him packing. The Arab world applauded; the oppressed saw a spark of hope. Europe and America stood in awe while Nasser became the brown giant of the Third World.

Then came the infamous tripartite invasion of Egypt on October 29, 1956, but Nasser held on to the Canal and the reins of power. Israel had unabashedly conspired with Britain and France to reverse the tide of Arab history and impose a new imperial regime on our world.

The 1956 invasion of Egypt ceased on November 6. That day, a new baby was born in the Khaled family. We called him Nasser in honor of President Nasser, to symbolize our first hour of victory since the defeat of 1948. Nasser was number twelve and the last child of Ali Khaled. Now the family could either form a soccer team or take on the "twelve tribes" of Israel. The decision was already made.

That autumn was the most exciting period of my childhood. We were engaged in all sorts of feverish activities. It seemed as if the whole school was one family, the whole of Sour was one tribe, the whole of the Arab world was one nation-state. It was a time to remember and enjoy, a time of pride and self-confidence. But the enemy was still at the gates.

The years from 1956 to 1959 were my period of political apprenticeship as an activist. Although I had sensed intense political interest and activity in our house since 1954, I somehow did not grasp its full significance and was not really involved in the discussions.

Brother Mohammad was a member of the Arab Nationalist Movement, and he frequently gave us literature to distribute in Sour or posters to paste up. Sisters Zakiah and Rahaab must have joined the Movement in 1956 or 1957, and they were very active.

I began to associate with the Movement people in 1957. I didn't realize, however, how much more there was to the movement than writing, distributing pamphlets, demonstrating, or making speeches.

The Movement was active in 1957 when it was widely rumored that Turkey was planning to invade Syria and overthrow the progressive regime on behalf of the US. We had numerous discussions, but there was no organized youth movement to take action. I was on the periphery and asked my sisters for information, which they refused to give because I was not a fully fledged member of the Movement. However, my enthusiasm for associating with liberationists and my emotional commitment to the cause offset any misgivings I might have had about not being a participating member.

In 1958, under artillery fire from the Lebanese army, the distinction between member and non-member ceased. Sour was under siege. The false friends of Palestine and Arabism began to show their teeth immediately after the formation of the United Arab Republic in February 1958. To protect their own tottering regimes, the Hashemites of Iraq and Jordan formed their own counter-federation, probably under Western instigation.

The whole Arab world was polarized: pan-Arabism versus provincial sovereignties; revolution versus counterrevolution; Cairo versus Baghdad. In this political context, the Lebanese President Chamoun, the darling of Western diplomats, decided to seek a second presidential term. The Arab Nationalist Movement, as well as other forces, progressive and reactionary, sought to block the constitutional amendment proposed by his party.

Because of the constitutional deadlock, the conflict of antagonistic social forces, and the opportunism of merchants and politicians on both sides, a civil war erupted on May 10, two days after the assassination of Nasib Al-Matni, a renowned Arab political editor.

In Sour, local opposition to the Arab Nationalist Movement was feeble. It was easy for us to seize the city and run its government in the interests of the people and the rebellion. The Island of Sour proper was under our absolute control. However, the army held the gate at the northern end of town, where the opposition had numerous followers, including the local member of parliament, his tribe, and its clients.

Tempers in Sour had been running high since April 2, 1958, when the gendarmerie had shot and killed Maan Halawah, a prominent nationalist leader. Most people in Sour considered his murder unwarranted and unprovoked. The Solidarity Club of Sour, however, interpreted Halawah's murder as a declaration of war on the Arab Nationalist Movement as well as an attempt by the Lebanese authorities to intimidate the city and foil the nationalists. Their premonitions proved correct.

A three-day curfew was imposed, followed by a round-up of "political agitators." When the people discovered what was happening, they broke the curfew, stormed the police station, and released the prisoners. This time, Mohammad Kassem, another distinguished nationalist, was killed, and I had my first brush with death, escaping by only a few centimeters.

Although I had participated in practically every demonstration in Sour for the past six years (1952 until April 1958), it still seemed like just a lot of fun. I had not seen anyone murdered since the man who died in front of our house in Haifa when I had been safely hidden under the staircase. Maan Halawah, however, was gunned down by the Lebanese gendarmes while shouting nationalist slogans as he was raised shoulder high by comrades. Mohammad Kassem was shot when the gendarmes tried to re-impose their curfew on Sour. I was by his side, handing him stones to hurl at the gendarmes when he was cut down.

I ran screaming for help. When help came, he was still alive, and we rushed him to the hospital in a broken old car. I thought he was going to live. The surgeon came out of the operating room after a few minutes. He walked slowly towards us, then solemnly offered his condolences, trying to hide his own tears. For the first time in my life, I knew the loss of a comrade in battle. I cried for days.

The city mourned the loss of two great comrades and gave them heroes' funerals. But that was only the beginning. The summer of 1958 was a summer of mourning. The paramilitary forces and the army of Chamoun advanced like a pack of mercenaries to ravage our city and bring us the blessings of American weaponry.

That summer, I do not remember sleeping a whole night without interruption, for I was a soldier at thirteen, and I had sentinel duty and other political and military obligations. I was anxious to be a good soldier.

As the Lebanese divided and brother killed brother, it became evident that too many foreign fingers were on the triggers. On July 16, 1958, American Marines landed in Lebanon, two days after the Iraqi people overthrew the Hashamite dynasty there and executed Nuri al-Said and Abdul-Ilah, Britain's most faithful Arab agents. The Lebanese-Arab people witnessed the awesome majesty of the sixth fleet. Unhappily, however, for America, it was too late to restore Nuri and company to power. But they stayed in Lebanon, deadlocked the civil war, and declared it a draw. Arab political commentators wrote books on "Neither Victorious Nor Vanquished."

Fortunately, the summer of 1958 in Sour was not as devastating as we had feared. The destruction was mitigated by an uneasy, unwritten local accord with the army: the ANM controlled the town center, the army held the outskirts of the city. The continuous bombardment of our positions was nerve-racking and frightening. In addition, the army frequently cut off food supplies. But we improvised and managed.

At one stage, our area was being starved and our men's morale was weakening because of the bombardment of the army and their own hunger. We had about ten kilos of flour at home, and I decided that I could bake enough bread for the men. But instead of baking it, I kneaded the entire ten kilos and fried the dough in olive oil. Now I could supply a regiment, not only a few dozen fighters. The image of a revolutionary Jesus blessing the fish and feeding the multitudes came to mind, but I performed no miracles.

The crucial part came when I delivered the bread to the lines. I was caught in the crossfire of the two sides; each thought I was the enemy, but apparently neither was prepared to gun me down.

I was amazed by the speed of the bullets as they buzzed by and was somehow surprised to see a real battle scene raging, particularly with me in its midst. Until then, I had thought that battles were like demonstrations. I quickly learned about battles and screamed to both sides to stop fighting because I only had bread on my tray, which I carried on top of my head, as befits a Palestinian maiden.

Fortunately, one of the comrades recognized me and signaled to his men to stop firing. I ran in his direction when he called my name and reached the hungry men safely.

Later, I learned another lesson of war. I was ready to choke any Lebanese soldier I could lay my hands on when one day a soldier walked into our house asking for a drink of water. I replied that I'd give him a drink of poison before I'd give him a drink of water. He seemed taken aback:

"Why would you do such a thing?" he asked.

I said, "Because you're murdering our men."

He smiled and cautiously replied, "Miss, if we had been aiming our bombardment at your men and city, the whole thing would have gone up in smoke by now. We have orders to fire, and we are firing, but we are not aiming. We merely fire to keep your men edgy and in place, hoping that they won't try to attack us or attempt to cross to our side of town. Tell your comrades to stay put; otherwise, we will be forced to wipe out the whole area."

Mother and I listened carefully. I told him he was a liar and he deserved to die of thirst and starvation as well. Mother relented and told me to give the soldier a drink in return for the good news he brought us. I reluctantly did so, insisting that he was an enemy soldier and he should be treated accordingly.

"We should take him prisoner," I announced.

He gestured at his gun as he stood in the door, chuckling over my outrageous threats. He suggested that I try to attack his side of town if I were so courageous. Mother pleaded with him to tell his comrades not to fire so mercilessly on the city and men, and he in turn assured us that he was a Lebanese who loved his country and did not wish to see it destroyed.

In 1958, having proved my mettle in battle, I had earned the right to candidate membership in the Arab Nationalist Movement. My mother strongly disapproved of the political activities of the girls in the family. She felt that now that the civil war was over, the girls should stay at home and leave the politics to men.

Mother had no objections to brother Mohammad manning the trenches, staying out late at night, or going off on unknown political missions for weeks at a time. To her, Mohammad was a man, so he did the work of men. Such was her upbringing. She said she was also afraid of scandalous talk in the neighborhood about women in politics. Mother knew that social ostracism would result if any one of us stepped out of line.

My sisters assured her that they were mature and capable of looking after themselves. Besides, they said, the men they associated with were respectful, political gentlemen with high principles. None was out to violate any girl, especially girl comrades. Nothing would convince mother.

Father was a little reluctant and suspicious, but he favored our position, and it was finally he and Mohammad who came to the rescue. They succeeded in persuading mother not to disrupt the political work of my sisters. When we were kicked out of Palestine, they argued, Zionists did not distinguish between men and women. Women constituted over one half of the Palestinian people, and they too were exiled. The Israelis trained their women to fight and granted them civil liberties. If we wished to defeat the Israelis, we must outplay them in their own game.

Mother was silenced by one final question: "Do you wish to see Palestine liberated?" father asked.

"Yes," she said unhesitatingly.

Mohammad reasoned: "Mother, you cannot then oppose the participation of your daughters in political life, can you?"

Mother smiled. "I do not mind Zakiah and Rahaab joining," she relented, "but this child politician (referring to me) must stay at home."

I was the sacrificial lamb of the deal, but the right of women to participate was conceded. Since my sisters were allowed to participate in politics, it was inevitable that I should be allowed to do so eventually. In the meantime, I decided to continue my activities clandestinely.

In 1959, however, when Mother discovered that I had become a fully-fledged member of the ANM, she tried to forbid me from going to meetings. I couldn't very well offend her by flaunting my membership card. I told her that I was merely doing what I always did as a political supporter of the Movement, but Mother remained unconvinced.

On the night of a very important meeting, which I was determined to attend, I resorted to subterfuge. I took a bath and put on my pyjamas to convince Mother that I was not going anywhere that night. She must have thought that she had won the battle and that her "child politician" was recovering her senses.

As zero hour approached, I made my move and, still in my pyjamas, I went by Mother in the kitchen, saying casually, "I am a little bored, Mother, I am going to visit my girlfriend next door." She raised no objections. I headed directly to the meeting hall at the Solidarity Club.

My pyjama debut startled the members as I made my way to an empty seat. They were shaken by what they regarded as immoral behaviour. I was blasted for violating Arab decorum and polite womanly behaviour. They were almost ready to pass a motion of censure and perhaps expulsion. Some of the reactionaries thought my appearance in pyjamas was a tradition-trampling, sex-enticing episode. Tradition-trampling it might have been; sex-enticing it was not.

I was terribly disturbed by their male chauvinism and self-righteousness. I stayed through the meeting and left still angry because my commitment to the cause was not appreciated, and the personal difficulties I encountered at home were not taken into consideration.

How could we liberate Palestine and the Arab homeland if we ourselves were not liberated? How could we advocate equality and keep over half the female half of the human race in bondage? That would be the next battle waged at the Sour Solidarity Club. Mother never found out about this escapade, but she soon reconciled herself to my vocation and acceded to my political demands. It took the ANM nearly a decade to start tapping to the full the human reservoir of women.

The school of the Evangelical Churches was not equipped to provide schooling for the secondary school baccalaureates or beyond. I had to go elsewhere to continue my education. The Saida School for Girls was going to be my first opportunity to act completely on my own. I was excited by my newly won freedom as a young adult, but a little upset that school rules required that a student have two residential years to qualify for examination to the baccalaureate. That meant I was going to lose one of the two years I had gained when I started school. I thought repeating the fifth secondary grade was no tragedy and rationalized it as a splendid opportunity to do great political work.

But the autumn of 1960 was the year of the international summit at the UN, not the year of great power rivalry or regional wars. Everything seemed quiet and conducive to reflective prolonged study. President Nasser went to the UN; he looked tame compared to 1956. Diplomacy seemed to have replaced revolution; the Third World was coming of age, perhaps a little too soon. The only hot spot in the Arab homeland was Algeria. I had to adjust to a new social and political environment after the turbulent years of Sour and await the coming of a revolutionary messiah. He never came.

Palestine needed one, but the Popular Front was not born until November of 1967. In Saida, there was much time to spare and little action to engage in. Here I was no longer in a completely Palestinian enclave. This school was highly apolitical—a graveyard for a revolutionary.

I was placed in a house with twelve other girls. A few were Palestinians with whom I thought I could communicate. But to them, Palestine was in the distant and remote past. They wanted to obtain an "education" and find husbands. What a travesty of womanhood. I did not give up hope, however, and tried to accommodate myself to their mode of living.

I was convivial by nature and loved to be with people, but I felt somewhat lonely in the midst of these eleven girls. I took heart when I noticed another lonely person. Her name was Miss McNight, an American black who had come all the way from America to teach in a private school in Saida. I was a little startled at first until I learned the reason for her choice.

In Lebanon, she was treated as a person and given the deference we accord teachers in the Arab world; in America, she was regarded as a coloured woman, an inferior, perhaps even a sex object. Miss McNight and I quickly became good friends. It was natural for two strange black women in Saida to pool their resources and offer each other aid and comfort.

Miss McNight was a darling of a woman—vivacious, always smiling, quick witted the model of a big sister for me. But our politics differed. She was surprised when I expressed deep hatred of the Jews and taught me not to make sweeping declarations. She pointed out that not all Jews were Zionists; some were, in fact, anti-Zionist. I reflected on her distinctions and tried to adopt them into my thinking.

The anniversaries of the Balfour Declaration (November 2) and the Partition of Palestine (November 29) were approaching. The time came to test who stood where on my campus. I started to agitate for a general strike of schools, Sour style, to commemorate the anniversaries.

In Sour, my school was always in the lead. We used to commence the marches and force all the other schools to close down and join in the demonstrations. It was not to be fulfilled in Saida. Miss McNight appreciated the idea, but even she didn't like the idea of a general strike, the forced closing down of schools, the holding of massive public rallies, or the storming of police stations. She was a graduate of Martin Luther King's school of non-violence. She stood for prayer and the education of the enemy. I was a militant revolutionary who was born in the crucible of revolutionary upheaval. Despite our differences of opinion, Miss McNight and I remained friends.

As a member of an oppressed race, she was sympathetic to my cause. She used her influence to persuade the Lebanese Arab principal to let me hold on Arab soil a peaceful student rally in support of the Palestinian cause. The principal only agreed reluctantly, thinking she was doing a favor to her neighbors from Palestine. The rally, however, was postponed from November to May 15, 1961, the thirteenth anniversary of the Zionist state. Then I delivered my first public lecture on Palestine.

I spoke of the history of Palestine and Zionism and my hopes for the future. Zionism, as a political concept, came to the fore at the turn of the twentieth century. It was at the outset a religious idea—old Jews pilgrimaged to Jerusalem to spend their last days there and die in the holy land. Zionism, as a word, was coined in 1886 by

Ben Acher, a European Jew who had never been to Palestine.

It was Herzl who started the political side of Zionism in his pamphlet *The Jewish State*. He was an Austrian, assimilated Jew who cared very little about Jewry prior to the 1880s.

As a political correspondent covering the Dreyfus trial in Paris, he was converted to Zionism. He was appalled that France, the most civilized nation in Europe, was blatantly persecuting a fellow Jew and making him a scapegoat for a crime he never committed. Herzl felt that only in a Jewish state could the Jew become a "normal" person and lead a life of inner peace.

He used all his energies and capitalist contacts to mobilize European Jewry and convened them at the first Zionist congress in 1897, at Basle. His program was adopted, and the World Zionist Organization was formed with Herzl as chairman.

Herzl sought aid from the Kaiser to realize his dream. He journeyed to Istanbul and sought the aid of the Sublime Porte. He told his prospective patrons that Jewish capital, knowledge, and skill would be placed at the disposal of Berlin and Istanbul if the Porte granted access to the Jews in the southern part of Arabia, Syria, and Palestine. However, the Porte, fearing the reaction of his Arab subjects, was unable to confer such a title.

Herzl was forced to look elsewhere for allies. He found one in Britain, the colonial power that occupied Egypt, the Sudan, and the Arab Gulf. He repeated his offer to the British and argued that a Jewish state would be a great bulwark against Arab revolution and a local sentinel to guard Britain's vital interests in the area, which included the Suez Canal and the trading routes to the Far East.

From the very beginning, the idea of an Israeli state was sold to the Western powers as a wedge to keep the Arabs divided. The British appreciated the proffered cooperation of the international Jewish bourgeoisie and offered such land areas as Argentina and Uganda where the Jews could settle.

Although Herzl preferred a Jewish state in Palestine, he accepted the Uganda offer and sold it to his compatriots at the World Zionist Organisation congress of 1903. Shortly afterwards, Herzl died, and the Uganda project was buried. Britain also offered Al-Arish in Egypt on the Mediterranean Coast, the area nearest to Palestine, and that proposal was turned down by the Zionist diehards.

(In the autumn of 1971, Israel controlled not only the whole of Palestine, but also Al-Arish, Sinai, and the Golan Heights of Syria.)

Zionist colonies were set up in Palestine, and thousands of Jews were filtered in because of the incompetence and corruption of the Ottoman administration. By 1917, when the Zionists extracted the Balfour Declaration from the British, the Jews constituted less than ten percent of the population of the area. However, the draftees of the Declaration had the temerity to refer to our people as the "non-Jewish population" rather than referring to the Jews as a minority that could have religious rights in Palestine.

The British were powerful and liked to have powerful friends with capital. The Zionists were prepared to pay any price, make any deal, offer every conceivable sacrifice, and commit any crime to reach their goal. They did, and in 1948, Israel was established over the corpse of the Palestinian people.

With the diplomatic support of the great powers, they were able to attain their objective quickly because Britain and France divided the Arab East among themselves into seven states and imposed on the Arabs a so-called "sacred trust" of civilization under Western tutelage. Then the allies suppressed the Arab National Movement and crushed the revolutionary elements that launched the Great Arab Revolution of 1916.

Much more significantly, Britain allowed the Zionists to establish dual power in Palestine and denied the same privilege to the Arabs. The cards were stacked in favor of Zionism.

To undo this conspiracy, we revolted on a number of occasions against the mandate and Zionist colonization and fought for our national independence. But the enemy was in our ranks, and our own ruling class was finally responsible for our betrayal.

The 1936 General Strike was a classic example in which the peasants and workers led the revolution and forced the upper class to join forces with them. They did, but only to abort and sacrifice the revolution on the altar of personal advantage.

When the war of 1948 came, our ruling class had abandoned us to the wind. We were leaderless, dispersed, and on our own. The Zionists plucked the land from our hearts with little cost and less effort.

The bankruptcy of our feudal leaders and the collapse of our social structure ushered in the age of the colonels' regimes—regimes that were progressive, reformist, and Arabist. Meanwhile, the Zionists proceeded to establish a racist, exclusive society where East European Zionists, Polish and Russian, dominated the government, political parties, trade unions, bureaucracy, and business. Afro-Asian Jews were the target of discrimination, class exploitation, and European contempt. The Arab inhabitants, the rightful owners of Palestine, were placed under military administration and used along with the Arab Jews as a cheap labor supply.

I concluded with a plea to free Palestine. Such a state of affairs cannot continue, and we must not allow it to continue. We can end it through Arab unity and the liberation of Palestine.

Our goal can be reached if the UAR is expanded and all the Arab states become one nation-state. We must fight for one Arab nation, for unity, for freedom, for socialism. We must defeat enemy number one, America, the supplier of Hawk missiles to Israel, and we must seize our own oil resources.

We must learn to emulate our Algerian brethren in order to liberate Palestine. Long live Palestine, Arab and revolutionary!

The students applauded heartily; they seemed to have been favorably impressed by my knowledge of Palestinian history and my commitment to unity. At that moment, neither I nor they foresaw the breakup of the UAR on September 28, 1961, when Syria withdrew, thereby dashing the Arab hope for unity and forcing the Palestinian people to reexamine their whole strategy of liberation. The breakup of the UAR was the temporary collapse of hope, and yet it also brought about the rise of a Palestinian revolutionism.

Palestinian organizations of all sorts suddenly sprang up everywhere and mushroomed in the next three or four years. A new age dawned in the Arab East while the Arab West inched its way to independence in Algeria through armed struggle.

That spring, I obtained my secondary school baccalaureate and went back to Sour for the summer, hoping to go to AUB in the autumn if I passed the entrance examinations. Sour was the vortex of nationalism that summer, and every conceivable question regarding the future of Arabism was raised and debated.

The Movement was in disarray, but we took heart because Nasser was building rockets and fleets. On July 23, 1962, Nasser celebrated the first decade of the Egyptian revolution by displaying "Egyptian"-made rockets, ships, tanks, and planes. He announced to the world that Egyptian rockets would reach just to the south of Beirut. He and Amer saluted the parade and acted as if they were Stalin, Churchill, and Roosevelt combined.

We were elated; at last, all of Israel was within the firing range of Arab rocketry. Nasser also declared that Egypt's fleet was the greatest in the Eastern Mediterranean, and we felt the time may have come to take revenge even on Turkey for her butcheries of the First World War.

In the summer of 1962, I once again had to face the problem of being a Palestinian Arab woman. My sisters in the West speak of two kinds of oppression: class and sexual. I had to face four kinds of oppression: national, social (the weight of traditions and habits), class, and sexual.

At this point, I was particularly prone to oppression because I was a woman. My family professed equality like most modern families but didn't practice it. Although I passed the baccalaureate examination with flying colors and my brother Khaled failed, my family insisted on sending him to university instead. I was a very low priority item compared to my brothers.

I was finally able to attend the American University of Beirut in 1962-63 due to the generosity of my brother Mohammad, who was working as an engineer in Kuwait. I scored the second-highest average at the AUB entrance exam: eighty-seven percent, which should have entitled me to a scholarship, but for some reason or other, I was not given one.

But I was delighted to have passed and wanted to enroll as quickly as possible before I got railroaded into some uncreative role like office work or marriage and baby production.

When I arrived in Beirut in late August of 1962, my earthly possessions consisted of fifty Lebanese pounds. I thought I could register on the installment plan. The AUB registrar, however, didn't believe in that basic American principle. I did all I could to persuade him to let me register before my place was taken by someone else; I promised to pay the balance before the beginning of the academic year. He wouldn't budge.

But a girl in the office sympathized with me. "How will you raise the balance for your fees, Miss?" she asked.

"I have a brother in Kuwait who promised to send me to university if I passed the examination, and I did," I was quick to explain.

"Go and telegraph your brother," she instructed. I ran to downtown Beirut and telegraphed Mohammad. The cost was twelve pounds. I now had only thirty-eight Lebanese pounds. I realized how quickly I could blow the money and end up penniless and unregistered.

I waited and waited, and a whole day elapsed before word came that the money was coming. I smiled to myself with satisfaction. My brother, like all good Arab men, honored his promises. I flew back to AUB and proudly presented the registrar with my fees. He uttered a few bureaucratic words, and I was registered.

At AUB, I enrolled in the four required freshman courses: chemistry, Arabic literature, English, and math. Only one of my four professors was of Arabic origin, and I couldn't tell the difference between him and his three other fellow professors. They were all American in outlook, behavior, and manners. They were pseudo-Ivy

Leaguers in a provincial school that only excelled in producing CIA spies and ministers. I don't know which was the lesser evil of the two.

My nominal education was taking place at AUB; my real education was in the lecture hall of the Arab Cultural Club of Beirut and in the ranks of the ANM.

At the ACC, I became acquainted with distinguished Arab intellectuals such as Joseph Mogheizel, the club's president, and Mohsen Ibrahim, the editor of Al-Hurriyah, then the official voice of the Arab Nationalist Movement. I also met Teysier Koubaa, the president of the General Union of Palestinian Students (GUPS). The group of students and intellectuals I met in that academic year now occupy leadership roles in the Popular Front and the Arab left.

AUB was an intellectual graveyard for me. It was a "finishing" school for the rich children of the Middle East and a social club for the colonial elite of the Arab world. Student government was banned, and the university was run like an American corporation. Students whose fees were not paid in full were often forbidden to attend classes. The only permissible activities on campus were dances, parties, and plays. No open political clubs were allowed. There were no demonstrations, no political rallies, and no guest speakers.

I lived at Jewett Hall, the women's residence, where I had an American roommate named Judy Sinninger. Her social life never ceased to amaze me. One week, she had three different dates with three different men, and she kissed each one of them with the same passion in the grand room at Jewett in front of a lot of other girls. I asked Judy how she could do it. She passed it off, "It was all nice, clean American fun with no strings attached." I laughed and admired her for her amorality.

But Judy and I were more than roommates. We were intellectual companions. She lectured me on American government, values, and social order, and I lectured her on the Arabs. She was a liberal Kennedy fan; I was a Nasser admirer.

The test of our friendship came in October 1962, a decisive month in America and the Arab world. On October 22, 1962, Kennedy threatened to invade Cuba unless the Soviet missiles were dismantled and removed from Cuba. On October 2, the UAR had officially sent its troops to Yemen to bolster the republican regime that had overthrown the medieval regime. Judy and I had long and heated dialogues concerning these events. The dialogues were mutually instructive, but neither of us convinced the other.

Judy held that it was right for America to demand the removal of missiles from Cuba. The missiles, she claimed, constituted a strategic threat to her country's national security. I considered it criminal and barbarous on the part of the United States to threaten atomic holocaust unless it got its own way.

Judy regarded the dispatching of UAR troops to Yemen as an invasion. I saw it as a moral obligation on the part of President Nasser, a noble gesture that he undertook to save the revolution from its corrupt enemies.

She asserted that Nasser was an ambitious politician who sought to seize the Gulf's oil and use it for his personal aggrandizement. I countered that we had a right to that oil and it should be used for the benefit of the Arab people. She saw Nasser's activities as part of a Soviet plot to occupy the Arab world. I explained to Judy that we were not fighting just to expel the colonial and neo-colonial powers from our region only to offer our homeland on a silver platter to a new superpower.

Judy was an imperial citizen, however liberal and idealistic she may have been. I was a Palestinian Arab woman without a homeland, living in exile in an American colony in Ras Beirut. She had everything to lose; I had everything to gain. One's social consciousness is indeed determined by one's social conditions.

Although politics were banned on campus and GUPS' (General Union of Palestinian Students) political activities were low-keyed, we engaged in confrontation politics in the spring of 1963. The proclamation of the Republic of Palestine based in the city of Nablus provided us with the occasion. Needless to say, Nablus, before and after the proclamation, remained under the firm control of King Hussein and his tribal soldiery. But there was a fair amount of agitation that reflected Palestinian dissatisfaction with Hussein, the Arab states, and the general social condition.

Moreover, new Palestinian organizations appeared on the scene, and by the autumn, the Arab states were forced to take notice and start talking about Palestinian unity. At AUB, we held demonstrations in support of Palestinian demands for a place under the sun. The administration initially turned a deaf ear to our activities, hoping that the spring offensive was a passing phenomenon.

We were prompted to move quickly by the widespread, accurate rumors that the Jordanian embassy had called in Palestinian students and threatened to cancel their Jordanian passports if they didn't cease their political agitation. We responded with more demonstrations, an action that gathered momentum rapidly, involving practically all the old politicos of Beirut and a significant proportion of foreign students.

This was the first time that foreign students at AUB had rallied to the cause of the Palestinians since 1948, when President Dodge had protested the establishment of the state of Israel to President Harry Truman of the United States and had been axed from his post for it.

The university administration braced itself for counteraction. Amidst an atmosphere of high tension, GUPS proposed that a student committee be formed to represent Palestinian students before the Jordanian embassy. The committee was formed, and a number of prominent foreign students were elected to the committee. I was included in the group.

The same day, we descended in full force on the Jordanian embassy and told the ambassador in no uncertain terms that we would slash his throat if he withdrew the passports. I did most of the talking, and my fellow students backed me to the hilt.

Moments after our arrival, the embassy was surrounded by the Lebanese gendarmes, and a whole contingent of what appeared to be armed intelligence service officers stormed into our meeting office. The ambassador seemed to know exactly what was happening, although he claimed not to have called in the police. In the presence of the whole committee, he had to eat his words and advise the police that we were not a gang of criminals, merely a committee of AUB students visiting his excellency. The guards surveyed each one of us and left the room.

I resumed the violent threats and insisted that we be given written assurances that passports wouldn't be canceled. The ambassador said that he was not instructed to give such assurances, but he was authorized to deny the report and give us his word of honor that such action was not contemplated. I sensed a feeling of victory and drank Arab coffee with the ambassador and assured him that we would be back if any action were taken against Palestinian students.

Since we were talking in English and I was being so forceful, he presumed that I was not an Arab. Before we left, I spoke to him in Arabic and assured him that I was an Arab, a Palestinian, and that every Arab woman was going to be my kind of woman in the near future. He smiled paternally and bid us farewell.

That same spring, I once again had to face the problem of being a woman. The ANM decided to train the first paramilitary contingent of university students. I was among the first to apply, and I couldn't be turned down on some flimsy excuse because of my revolutionary credentials and my long experience as an activist. Moreover, since I was on the executive committee of GUPS and a militant from AUB, they were afraid to turn me down.

Instead, they tried to persuade me not to go because of the harshness of the weather, the physical fatigue, and the embarrassment my presence would cause. I assured them I was prepared to face and overcome all these difficulties. They finally agreed to let me go, and I underwent the necessary training.

Politics were banned on campus, but the ANM was organized as a secret organization on a cell basis. I had the responsibility of distributing literature at Jewett Hall and pasting posters on trees in the area. I did it secretly, towards five o'clock in the morning or about one a.m. before I went to bed.

One night, I was caught by a watchman who, at first, appeared severe and threatening, but who turned out to be a member of our underground. It was quite a rewarding experience to find a comrade in the middle of the night. From then on, he provided me with information regarding security and advised me when it was safe to work. Being caught meant expulsion without trial.

Inside Jewett Hall, I was on my own. I placed bundles of literature in the women's mailboxes and simultaneously, periodically denounced those who imposed on us that useless literature. Occasionally, a student or two would come to the defense of the distributor, arguing that it was essential for us to know what was happening and to hear all points of view. This tactic helped me in organizing and also to know which students were politically inclined.

I was never revealed as a nationalist and a member of the underground to the students as a whole, but the administration was clever, and they suspected that I was the torchbearer of nationalism at Jewett. I was called to the dean's office when I was seen publicly distributing literature relating to the fifteenth anniversary of Israel. The dean spoke to me in quick, angry, Americanized English, which I pretended not to understand. She was outraged that an AUB student couldn't speak English.

She called in a secretary and asked her to act as an interpreter. The dean demanded, "Did you read the student handbook?"

"Yes, I did," I replied through the interpreter.

"Did you know that according to article six, you could be expelled for distributing political literature without permission?"

"Yes," I said.

"Why did you do it then?"

I innocently replied that what I was distributing was not political literature at all. She took the pamphlet from the secretary's hand and read a few passages out loud.

"Isn't this a political pamphlet that comes under rule six?"

I said I didn't know what a pamphlet was and that I didn't know what she was talking about anyway. The poor liberal dean started explaining to me that a political pamphlet was a statement that explained, defended, and advocated a political position. I agreed that her definition was excellent but contended that it didn't apply in this case because Palestine and her defense were natural and essential to me.

"Palestine is not politics to me," I declared. "It is a question of life and death, and no one, certainly no Yankee who can't even speak Arabic, can tell me how to act on the issue and how to fight for my country."

The dean considered me a recalcitrant student who needed discipline, and she threatened to expel me.

"I dare you to do so!" I screamed in English and declared war on her as a CIA agent and on AUB as the servant of the Pentagon and the oil cartels. "Yankee dean, there will come a time when I will be sitting in your chair, and I will expel all of your kind."

I stormed out of her office shouting, "Long live Palestine, long live the ANM, long live the revolution!" The dean was shocked and probably had to take a few tranquilizers before settling down to a day of bureaucratic business.

In the spring of 1963, I passed my freshman year, although not with distinction. I had hoped to return to university and continue my education, but money was not available, and I had to look for work. The temporary ending of my schooling made me reflect on the value of my education in general.

My academic education was, on the whole, meaningless. It taught me nothing of lasting value. The few sparks of life in these years were all related to the politics of revolution and were outside the curriculum.

In the first three or four years of my education, I enjoyed reading history and literature. Towards the end of my student career, my interests shifted to mathematics and chemistry, and I began planning to specialize either in pharmacology or agriculture. Agriculture was vital because when we returned to Palestine, we would need to cultivate the land on a scientific basis and prove to the world that we could make better use of it than the Zionists.

During the first three years of secondary school, I read about important figures: Lincoln, Napoleon, Hitler, and Lenin. I admired them all in the beginning. At the moment, I admire Lincoln as a liberal in his time, Lenin as the greatest "historic world individual," to be followed only by Mao, Ho, and Guevara. At first, I admired Hitler because I thought he was the enemy of the Jews. Later, I found out he classified Arabs as subhumans, only slightly above the gypsies and the Jews. I admired Napoleon's military conquests and his ability to overcome all obstacles until I discovered that he did it all for personal glory.

In literature, I read excerpts from Dickens and Shaw. I loved their work and once tried to imitate Shaw in an essay. The teacher didn't appreciate the effort, and the C plus was a powerful deterrent to further imitation. I dismissed Shakespeare as a pompous circumlocutionist. In Arabic literature, I liked the poets of the Umayyad and Abbasid periods. That's all the "education" I remember. Since I had plenty of time to spare in 1960-61, I read Gandhi on my own. I liked his moral integrity, but I felt that he was born a slave and never transcended his slavery.

As to personal and social relations, I led a "normal" life for an Arab girl. For six years, I liked a fellow Palestinian student of peasant background. At first, his careful avoidance of girls provoked my curiosity. Later, I discovered his dislike of women stemmed from watching his mother being raped by Israeli soldiers as they were fleeing from the Safad area in 1948. He abandoned his mother the moment he was able to subsist on his own.

I haven't seen Adel since I went to AUB, and I wonder whether he is among our fighters or whether he is one of our martyrs. Perhaps he has abandoned hope altogether and is living in the slums of some Arab town.

I've had casual boyfriends but never became really attached to any man. The older I grew, the more attached I became to the revolution.

# 3 Exile in Kuwait

In Kuwait and the Arab Gulf, every non-Kuwaiti is an alien, except the British, the Americans, and their appendages.

Katib Karouni: ARAB NATIONALISM WAS A NINETEENTH-CENTURY IDEA. It was first propounded by literary elements and liberal writers who came in close contact with European thought and writers at British and French universities. Students and reformers were the first to espouse the nationalist ideas and organize Arab clubs. From the outset, Arab intellectuals were in the forefront. Arab soldiers and officers in the Ottoman armies joined the intellectuals at the turn of the century, particularly after the Ottomans launched their Turkification policy in the first decade of this century.

In those days, nationalists did not have a clear conception of nationalism, nor did they have a defined framework encompassing all the Arabic-speaking people. Nationalism was "Eastern," not Western. That is, it included the fertile crescent states of West Asia, not North Africa. Indeed, some important figures, such as Al-Afghani, who advocated the "Islamic Baath," failed to distinguish between Arabism and Islam. His concept was strengthened by Western encroachments on the region and complicated by his advocacy of liberal democratic ideas within the Moslem world.

Al-Afghani and his followers regarded the problems facing Islam as ones of civilization and community. They thought that the Napoleonic invasion of Egypt (1798) and the subsequent takeovers of the Arab West by France and the occupation of Egypt by Britain were a repeat of the medieval wars of Islam and Christendom. To them, the answer was therefore clear: the Moslem world had to react as a community to withstand that onslaught and to defeat the West. Arab and Moslem were one; all Moslems had to act collectively. It took nearly three decades to jettison that mental albatross: Islam and Arabism were divorced and distinguished as two different concepts, rather than remaining as one and indivisible.

The occasion for the separation was revealing. It left the Arabs breathless, defensive, bared. They knew how to react to the "Christian" West and how to face the latter's challenge — by holy war.

Now their co-religionists, the Turks, tried to Turkify the Arab East, which they had dominated from the sixteenth century until World War I.

The Arab response was anguished shock. They had to learn quickly that Muslims were not all brothers and that Turks were not Arabs; that the world was no longer run by religious bigots but by capitalists; that states and parties seek alliances on the basis of mutual interests, not religious affiliations; that Arabs must alter their view of the world or remain subjugated. There was no specific party to cope with these issues. But there were individuals and groups based in Beirut, Cairo, and Damascus. There were also the nationalist officers in the Ottoman army who formed a part of the "Young Turks."

These officers were treated contemptuously by the rest of the "Young Turks" after the latter disclosed their intentions in 1908 and repudiated the idea of a decentralized empire based on national autonomy. Those officers, the intellectuals, and students constituted the cadres of the Great Arab Revolution in 1916.

The net result of that revolution was the proclamation of a Damascus-based Arab state in 1920. The revolution and its leaders were rapidly suppressed and dispersed. The "Eastern" part of the Arab world was dismembered and occupied by the British and French, who divided it among themselves in accordance with the Sykes-Picot treaty, which allocated Lebanon and Syria to France, and Iraq, Palestine, and Transjordan to Britain. The secular Arab nationalists were eliminated; the regionalists were bribed by state principalities and given kingly titles; the Hashemites and their hangers-on carried the day by becoming pliable British tools, using religion and tribalism to perpetuate their power. The idea of nationalism alone survived as the Arab East was divided into spheres of influence between Britain and France. Palestine was conferred on the Zionists in the Balfour Declaration, and the mandate's regime did its utmost to realize the Zionist ideal.

To infuse the idea of nationalism with socialist content required approximately half a century of turmoil and at least three major defeats for the prevailing feudal and petit bourgeois regimes. In each case, the Zionists triumphed while digging their own graves deeper. From 1920 to 1948, nationalists attempted to advance a secular liberal idea of nationalism. They failed dismally because both they and the feudal commercial ruling classes thought in terms of the Western capitalist analysis and tried to compete for Western favors; both were imposed practically from above, and they were never able to incorporate the masses into their system. The secular nationalists, with their liberal beliefs, had the historic value of discrediting themselves and (the Wafd party of Egypt) unwittingly convincing the Arab people that the West was their intractable enemy. In other words, the Arabs remained weak and divided, and the West was held responsible for their division and penury. It seemed, moreover, that the West never gave its clients an opportunity to develop a capitalist society in the Arab world, and the Arab rulers remained as remote from the people as their Ottoman predecessors. In this environment of weakness, Zionism was able to implant itself and deliver the coup de grâce to Arab feudal mercantilism in 1948. As a result, a petit bourgeois nationalism arose and reflected itself in the first pan-Arab nationalist party—the Baath, a social democratic movement.

The Arab Baath (formed between 1943 and 1947), as opposed to the Islamic Baath of yesteryear, was a significant development. It revitalized the idea of Arab nationalism and gave it a secular frame of reference. More importantly, however, the Baath tied the idea of Arab unity with the concept of socialist humanism and placed socialism anew on the agenda of the Arab nation. The slogans of Baath were liberty, unity, socialism. Unfortunately for Baath, it did not inherit the mantle of the Arab revolution because its ideologies did not take into account the contradiction between liberal democracy and socialism, because they glossed over the relationship between socialism and mass mobilization and organization, and because the leadership preferred individualist theorizing and rulers to relevant social theory and mass work.

Since Baath was born an adolescent intellectual, it was unable to surmount that condition and integrate itself into the society it purported to represent. In the sixties, its military leaders became putschists and incapable of relying on the masses; the colonels depended on their fellow colonels and the civilians on their tribal associations, and the intellectuals on their salon audiences. Baath became only a party in name in the 1970s, not a revolutionary instrument for the transformation of Arab society.

To a number of nationalists, Baath lost its historic relevance in the late 1940s because Palestine was not its first priority and because it lacked an understanding of revolutionary struggle and iron Organisation. Those nationalists attempted to replace Baath as the historic agent of Arab social change, and in 1948, they formed the Corps of Arab Martyrdom (Kataib El-Fidaa El-Arabi). Between 1952 and 1957, they were known as Arab youths (El-Shabab El-Arabi). In 1952, they called themselves the Arab Nationalist Movement (Haraket El-Komeen El-Arab). In 1967, they effectively ceased to exist. In 1970, the Arab Work Socialist Party (Hozib El-Amal El-Ishtiraki El-Arabi) succeeded the ANM as the Pan-Arab party. The Popular Front for the Liberation of Palestine (El-Jabhan El-Shaebeah Litahrir Filistine), which was formed in November 1967, replaced the Palestinian branch of the ANM, which had been set up in 1962. At the outset, the Movement was a collection of sentimentalist rationalists, nourished by the ideas of Satish Al-Hussari, a writer who stressed the idea of nationality and based it on language and history only. In

1963, the Movement was in a state of flux; revolutionary radical nationalism was posed as the new alternative. The social question was becoming the focal point. It was this prospect and the intellectual and moral challenges it entailed that I pondered then as a member. The nuclei for the ANM were organized by a group of students and graduates from the American University of Beirut in the 1940s.

The most important figures were Dr. George Habash, Dr. Wadih Haddad, Hani El-Hindi, and

Ahmad El-Khatib. The initial cadres were mostly Palestinians who were appalled by the Arab disaster of 1948.

The creation of the Zionist state gave the Movement the necessary impetus for growth. The leaders were populists, anti-imperialists, ultra-nationalists. To them, nationalism and anti-imperialism were the principal preoccupations; Israel was the principal enemy; the Arab masses were the principal friends. Because of these political propositions, the young nationalists fought in the 1950s against entangling Western alliances, against the Hashemites in Jordan and Iraq, against Arab advocates of Western capitalist ideas. As the Movement evolved, Nasser attained stardom in the firmament of the Third World by concluding the famous Czech arms deal with the Soviet bloc and nationalizing Suez. In recognition of these achievements, the nationalists identified themselves with Nasserism and applauded its deeds for the next decade. At the time, it was patently clear that both Nasser and the ANM were natural allies; both believed in class collaboration and national unity; both held ambiguous ideas regarding cooperative socialism; both were elitists and statist in their conception of leadership and the role of the state in the economy. The only difference was that Nasser was in power and was unable to transcend his environment.

The ANM was not in power and, in due course, it turned against those very oligarchic ideas. Nasser was proud to react and manipulate pressures from East and West and boasted about being a pragmatic power-wielder. The ANM leaders, on the other hand, were Movement people. As such, they were more attuned than Nasser to the currents of modern thought and more capable of grasping and adapting to reality.

In the mid-1960s, they became advocates and practitioners of armed struggle and scientific socialism. Nasser died in 1970, a soldier-diplomat, not an advocate of people's wars. Meanwhile, during the period of close collaboration, contact between Nasser and the Movement was maintained via such nationalist Syrian officers as Saraj and the Egyptian political ideologue, Abu-Alnour. The relationship was cordial but paternalistic. Direct contact was made for the first time on November 21, 1961, when Hani El-Hindi, a Syrian radical member of the ANM, visited Nasser at the latter's request. El-Hindi raised some fundamental issues with Nasser regarding the Syrian secession and the future prospects of Arab revolution, but by that time, Nasser's interests had shifted to "Egyptian socialism." Dr. Habash, the Secretary

General of the ANM, met Nasser on April 11, 1964, and was favorably impressed by Nasser's formidable personality and his ability to master issues and people. The exchange was in a period of expansive dimensions for Arab nationalism, and Nasser seemed to have recovered from the agony of the Syrian divorce.

However, the meeting took place at a point when the roads to Jerusalem began to diverge radically and openly. Therefore, it may be important to underscore the fact that the ANM not only preceded Nasser and Nasserism in terms of time, but also it never became his permanent and supple tool, nor did it stop at Nasserism. We admit that the ANM was a staunch defender and ally of Nasserism in the stage of the national revolution—and we offer no apology for it. Moreover, the parting of ways, not the break with Nasser, came over the South Yemen question in the mid-sixties. Here was a situation that Nasser tried to contain and keep under his grip. He helped organize and promote the Front for the Liberation of Occupied South Yemen (Flossy), a group of British-oriented unionists and nationalists headed by Sanjaq. The ANM, on the other hand, recognized its own South Yemen Wing (the FLN) as the legitimate representative of the South Yemenese. Armed struggle commenced in the countryside, and the peasants were converted to the revolution while Flossy was enjoying the limelight and the glare of Cairo and negotiating compromises with the British.

Finally, the British were forced out, and the People's Republic of South Yemen was proclaimed in November of 1967.

Within a few days, the bubble of Flossy was punctured, and it passed from the scene. Nasserism was contracting and narrowing its horizons. The ANM revolutionism was replacing it by expanding its base and broadening its social views. In the post-June-War period, ANM

revolutionism became the magnet of the Arab masses—
the galvanizing force of the poor, the weak, and the
wretched of the Arab world. In a nutshell, the question
that posed itself was: who shall govern, the colonels or
the people? We in the Arab Work Socialist Party say the
people. That's why we contend that the revolution is
coming; that's why I became a full-time revolutionary.

In the spring of 1963, Israel was fifteen years old. Instead
of rekindling the Arab spirit and resuming its historic
mission after the breakup of the UAR, Nasserism was
becoming inward-looking, repressive, managerial.
Economically bourgeois, it became a spent force in
historical terms, the Yemen "intervention" (October
1962) and the National Charter of May 1962,
notwithstanding.

Statesmanship, economic progress, and political stability
were touted as the hallmarks of the Egyptian regime. The
UAR placed advertisements in the New York Times
inviting monopolistic investors to share in its profitable
state enterprises. Gone were the days when Nasser spoke
and Western industries came to a halt for lack of oil;
gone were the days when Nasser spun revolutionary
slogans and the Arab masses seized and burned
embassies; gone were the days when Western prime
ministers were treated like messenger boys and scoffed at
in public. Yet, in spite of this turnabout, we in the ANM
remained Nasser supporters until 1967.

The Nasserite social order consisted of a Charter that
promised a new UAR based on Islam, democracy, and
cooperation; recognized the dominant role of the state in
the economy; acknowledged the role of the "national
bourgeoisie"; conferred on workers and peasants half of

the parliamentary seats; granted employees an advisory role in the management of their fields, factories, and offices, and pledged to give them financial rewards based on profits made.

Nasserism was turning Egypt into a "paradise" of colonels, managers, and clerks. By 1965, he, with Heikalian frankness, told the second Palestinian National Congress that he had "no plan for the liberation of Palestine." Furthermore, Arab unity was revived in the spring of 1963 for about three months when Iraq, Egypt, and Syria agreed (April 17) to form a new and revitalized United Arab Republic. The unity talks were held in Cairo after the Baathists, the junior partners of Nasser of the 1958 United Arab Republic period, seized power in Iraq (February 8) and Syria (March 8). To bolster their regimes, the Baathists called for Arab unity and for cooperation among "the progressive forces."

Nasser could not ignore or oppose their call lest he be considered an anti-unity man. After the proclamation of the New UAR, however, the Baathists returned to their capitals and began to purge the Nasserites and finally removed them from power completely. In early July, Nasser showed his displeasure by releasing the recorded tapes of the talks to Al Ahram, the mouthpiece of the middle-class Egyptians. Heikal, the editor, serialized censored verbatim accounts and commented scathingly on the Baath, thereby signaling to the world that Nasser had no intention of proceeding with the autumn merger as scheduled.

The disclosures demonstrated two facts: first, that Nasser was unwilling to regard anyone as his equal, or subordinate Egyptian "national interests" to the common

Arab good, and secondly, that the Baathists were insincere, mistrusted Nasser, and viewed themselves as the successors to a dying Nasserism. In the ensuing years, Baathism too became a regime of colonels. This and other semi-fictional incidents puzzled, bewildered, and confused the ANM.

By the spring of 1963, I realized I would not be able to return to AUB in the autumn. I had to make a decision. There were few work prospects to explore. There were none in Lebanon. I was nineteen years old, and I was not looking for a husband to serve; I couldn't stay at home and vegetate. In that confusing spring, a family incident led me to seek refuge outside of Lebanon.

For fifteen years, my family had been exiled from our beloved homeland. Since a state of war existed between the Arab states and Israel, we had not seen a single relative from Haifa or Majdel El Karoum. Travel restrictions were too severe; bureaucratic red tape was overwhelming, and financial considerations were difficult to overcome. However, after prolonged and careful preparations, my father went to see his family in Jerusalem at the Mendelbaum gate. He waited for three days, but no one showed up. A few weeks later, a meeting was again arranged, but this time my father was paralyzed and not able to go.

Mother went without him. The meeting was a nightmare of barbed wire. When grandmother saw mother, she presumed her son must have died, and she collapsed. My aunts, my cousins, and mother carried on a teary dialogue for about an hour. Little or nothing was said beyond conveying greetings and fleeting reminiscences. We were all drenched with tears. We looked at each other, wondering whether reunion would ever be possible; no one could utter a coherent sentence; we parted infuriated at the Zionist overlord.

As mother said adieu to grandmother, granny placed her necklace around mother's neck and kissed her. An Israeli guard looked on and instantly pounced on mother and snatched the necklace from her chest. Mother fought back, but the man with the gun prevailed. She returned home upset by Arab inability to protect her and shocked by Zionist brutality. Such events kept my family and most Palestinians away from the Zionists. Since then, we have not seen our relatives, and father died without having seen his mother and sisters for eighteen years.

What was I to do in the midst of this situation? Where was I to go? If I couldn't bend heaven, I would scratch hell; Kuwait was the only outlet.

There was no other possibility.

In the summer of 1963, the Voice of the Arabs beamed broadcasts from Cairo to the four corners of the globe, and the press of the Arab world was filled with the idea of the Palestine entity.

Innumerable Palestinians, including myself, were attracted to the idea, if not to the organization that was intended as its embodiment: The Palestine Liberation Organization (PLO). The PLO was set up by the Arab League States in January 1964. The PLO was launched by the Arab League to contain the Palestinians while supposedly giving them an instrument of liberation. At the time, only a few perceptive people saw Arab summitry for what it was. Those who foresaw had no power.

Arab presidents and kings met in the splendor of Cairo, and although they decided not to confront Israel, they led their people into believing that they were preparing for the eventuality of war. They issued joint military commands that had no power. Weeks later, they blamed their failure on Lebanon for allegedly not allowing Arab troops to occupy strategic positions on its soil, as if Syria and Jordan had agreed to the proposal and implemented it, and as if Lebanon had remained the only obstacle. They had allocated the astronomical sum of $13 million to divert the waters of the Jordan, yet such a sum wouldn't be enough to dig a ditch; they created the PLO as a crumb to the Palestinians, and the faithful believed in the good faith of the leadership.

All was a sham, as the disasters in June were unmistakably to show. The PLO was born crippled, if not dead, and the Arab states neither allowed the Palestinians to act independently nor did they themselves act with sufficient vigor to safeguard Palestinian interests. The PLO consisted of the remnants of a dead social class, and its leaders were given their positions in recognition of their loyalties to the various summit conferences. The PLO was a skeleton put on display at the Arab League headquarters; it was neither a revolutionary spearhead to lead the struggle for the liberation of Palestine nor a rallying point for the dispersed masses of "refugees."

In late September 1963, I departed for Kuwait with mixed feelings and without the prospect of employment. For three months, I was without work, waiting for a reply to my application from the Kuwait Ministry of Education. At last, I received word in mid-December that a position was available in Al Jahrah, some fifty kilometers from Kuwait City, the capital of the Kuwaiti state, where my brother Mohammad lived.

During the intervening three months, I thought about the world situation and pondered the meaning of life, especially after the assassination of President John F. Kennedy on November 22. I do not know why the Kennedy assassination affected me emotionally. Kennedy was the president of a state that helped perpetuate my exile, a state that maintained and advanced the Zionist cause I hated.

Kennedy was a sophisticated patrician, a class enemy, and he had given key posts in his regime to at least three dedicated Zionist Jews. He also approved the invasion of Cuba in April 1961 by a pack of America-supported mercenaries. Yet I, the hardened Palestinian revolutionary, for some inexplicable reason, cried when I heard the news. I watched the funeral on TV and saw Americans weep. Until then, I had thought of the United States as a nation of monsters and scoundrels capable of perpetrating every conceivable crime.

I revised my view slightly, but Lyndon Johnson's rapacity and Nixon's hypocrisy have reinforced the original image. I wept for Kennedy perhaps because I somehow identified with the youth of America that loved and admired him dearly. Perhaps I may have believed, as some Arabs did, that Kennedy was indeed going to work for the restoration of Palestinian rights, as the Kennedy-Nasser correspondence later illustrated. I suspect that my tears were a natural human reaction; my prejudices couldn't stop them until it was too late. I am not sorry I cried.

Al Jahrah for a girl from AUB and the political mill of Beirut was the city of eternal boredom. We were all "foreigners" in the eyes of the Kuwaiti Arab government, though every one of us came from the Arab world. The only colorful aspect of the school was the multitude of "foreign" dialects spoken. The Egyptians, Palestinians, and Syrians were the largest group. This was the first time I had come into close contact with Egyptians. The Syrians were the same as the Palestinians, with the exception of the lady principal, Souad, who excelled as an obsessive bureaucrat and an arbitrary woman. She was, to put it mildly, an administrator who prostrated herself before the Ministry of Education and set out to discipline her fellow teachers by a network of informers.

Matters were complicated for me because I had no conception of roles or rules. I knew of no distinctions between governors and governed; I had no idea of bureaucratic memos and no notion of external authority.

The only authority I had ever recognized since I left home in 1960 was that of the comrade regional commander. My world was turned upside down. My colleagues either delighted in my agony, resented me as proof of their cowardice, or secretly admired my rebellion. They were serfs who trembled before the knight and paid him homage.

At Al Jahraa, we could not leave campus without special permission during the week. On Thursday evenings, we could visit relatives or immediate family members and stay overnight. There were no cinemas to visit, no boyfriends to pass the time with, no British Museum to study in. Overt political activity was forbidden. We were truly family eunuchs in an oriental despotic order.

I recall distinctly the famous short sleeves episode when I opposed the authorities. The principal had threatened to expel me for appearing in short sleeves, which were banned in Kuwait despite the sweltering heat. I challenged her and threatened to expose my body further. She was infuriated but was unable to carry out her threat. I informed her that I would help her write a memo on my "scandalous" behavior to the ministry of education if she persisted in observing that ridiculous rule. She had to swallow her pride and wrote a memo recommending my transfer elsewhere at the end of the academic year. I exulted at the prospect, though I would regret the loss of the few friends I had made at Al-Jahrah.

The children at Al Jahrah manifested the cultural deprivation of a rural and remote Bedouin people, but they were intelligent and quickly absorbed information. Our school was the only window they had to the outside world. They needed to be taught the rudiments of living in their rapidly developing community and warned about urban slavery. Instead, I was teaching them English and science. But I used every possible opportunity to propagate my political cause. The pupils were susceptible and responded positively.

I did not reveal my association with the ANM: it would have been political suicide. The lady principal would have been delighted to invoke her powers. Instead, I injected my political virus in small doses. I related every issue to the world around us and, whenever possible, to the Palestinian question. Some pupils listened attentively; others patted their goats, sheep, or cows, or fed their chickens through the school windows. Their parents were not keenly aware of what was going on.

They thought the teacher knew best, and they in no way interfered with my work. The world of Al Jahrah had its good points; it was not all unpleasantness, particularly for those not politically inclined.

Spring came and found the Arab governments making noises about Israel "stealing" Arab waters from the Jordan River. They ostensibly made their own preparations to divert the river ten years too late. No military attempt to stop the Israelis was made. A few minor border incidents occurred, and the Arabs thundered revenge. The farce went on for a year or so. Israel freely carried out her diversion project and expropriated almost all the waters of the Jordan River.

Meanwhile, the honorable presidents and noble kings, without consulting the Palestinian people or considering other candidates, appointed Ahmed Shukairy chairman of the PLO. Shukairy was their man. He could be relied upon to make the necessary flamboyant pronouncements to appease the Palestinian masses, without precipitating a crisis or organizing the Palestinians into a fighting force. The PLO leadership was imposed from above and was accountable to the powers above, not to the Palestinian people whom it sought to represent.

Shukairy was touring in the Arab world, and he came to Kuwait to mobilize the Palestinians and get them to participate in a constituent assembly to elect a Palestinian parliament. In Kuwait, Shukairy contacted the people he knew—the former upper class of Palestine—who now held lower echelon positions in Kuwait as engineers or managers of small business enterprises. The children of the "refugees"—the school teachers, the skilled, semi-skilled, and manual workers—were not contacted; they were merely expected to applaud the "wise" decisions of the Arab leaders and rubber stamp the election of "their" representative, chosen from the "better" people. Moreover, since the Palestinians in Kuwait and throughout the Arab Gulf were permitted no organic community or viable organizations, it was very difficult accurately to determine communal feelings. This situation enabled certain self-seeking, self-appointed individuals to "represent" the Palestinians. In spite of all these difficulties and my own misgivings, I agitated on our campus, urging Palestinians to take an active part in forming branches for the PLO. But no branches were formed at Al Jahrah because too many people were skeptical. I shared the skepticism, but I thought the PLO was better than nothing at all since the Kuwait government recognized it as the official representative of the Palestinians and agreed to let Palestinians join it as long as they remained outside the Kuwaiti political arena.

My principal had received no directive to encourage such a club, and she decided the rule banning politics still applied and called me to her office to ask me to cease my activities. She argued that I was a Lebanese, I held a Lebanese passport, and had nothing to do with Palestine. I listened to her monologue without interrupting. When she finished, I stood up. "Woman principal, your kind of obedient, amoral, apolitical people were responsible for the loss of Palestine; your kind of careerists have oppressed the Palestinians more effectively than the Zionists have; your graveyard-like school has stunted the growth of intelligence; you are a part of the enemy camp. I believe if we don't overthrow your masters and your servile type, more tragedy and destruction will plague the Arab homeland. I believe you're more dangerous than the acknowledged foe. Let us suppose that I am only a Lebanese citizen. Does that 'nationality' absolve me of my Arab obligations? Does it erase my Arab identity? Does it mean that I am not an Arab woman?"

Principal, I am an Arab, I am a Palestinian, I am a Lebanese Arab who is going to proselytize the Arab cause here on your campus and everywhere. No force other than death can stop me. Act as you see fit. I shall not relent. I shall not be cowed. I shall not retreat. Good day." I walked out and slammed the door. I had made my last appearance in her office.

On May 28, 1964, the Palestine National Congress was opened in Jerusalem by King Hussein. Its three hundred and fifty delegates represented a cross-section of the Palestinian people, with traditionalists in the majority. A number of prominent "radicals" were barred from the Congress by the Jordanian authorities. The Congress elected an executive committee of seven, reconfirmed Ahmad Shukairy as chairman, issued a manifesto, the National Charter, which embodied the ideology of our bankrupt ruling class, and elected all sorts of high-sounding state committees to man the apparatus of the forthcoming "revolution." The PLO occupied the Palestinian seat at the Arab League headquarters in Cairo. Arab summitry continued in the autumn of 1964.

Within a year, the leaders themselves had stopped believing their own lies, though their media agents continued to expound the plans in purple prose and poetic visions.

In late June of 1964, I returned to Lebanon for what during the next six years became an annual furlough. In Lebanon, I rethreaded my way back to the underground and felt a sense of relief after the isolation of Al-Jahrah and the enervating heat of Kuwait. I observed that cracks were opening up within the citadel of the Arab Nationalist Movement in Beirut. However, these profound differences within the movement were frozen in the name of unity, good statesmanship, and personal relations.

Serious differences regarding ideology, strategy, organization, and personalities erupted again and again until a formal split was finally to take place in five years' time.

As autumn approached, I made plans to return to Kuwait. Once again, I had to live in the barracks, rather than with my brother. For a woman, living alone in Kuwait was simply unthinkable.

At the Shaab's school, I discovered that I had been demoted from the intermediate to the elementary level of teaching. I was confined to teaching grade two for the next five years and was thus deprived of my adolescent audience and the possibility of using my classroom as a political platform. Dismayed and annoyed at first, I reconciled myself quickly. There was nothing I could do to alter my teaching status. Resignation was a worse alternative since it meant being on the unemployment heap with a substantial number of other Arab workers.

My pupils were an enjoyable lot. Many of them were of Iranian origin; their parents had emigrated to Kuwait in pursuit of work. The Shaab's school was populated with working-class children who were anxious to learn and willing to do their homework. They were tireless children who could have outraced baby camels given the opportunity. They were a delight to be with, but they were not important as political converts.

Here, I had the opportunity to say anything in the classroom without feeling Big Brother was watching; the problem was to learn how to communicate with seven- and eight-year-olds and know what to expect from them. I decided it would be best not to expect anything more than the mastery of a few central Palestinian issues such as the Balfour Declaration, the Partition of Palestine, and the creation of Zionist Israel.

At the faculty level, there was little tension and no clashes with the principal or any other colleagues. From 1968 on, the principal and a large number of teachers supported the Fateh. Those of us who supported the Popular Front had no difficulty coexisting with them. But though the atmosphere was conducive to dialogue and hospitable to liberal democratic ideas, I never publicly revealed my true political affiliations. I was also helped because I had learned the rudiments of being a teacher and thus staved off confrontations with bossy administrators.

Kuwait City was a cosmopolitan center compared with Al Jahrah. We were not village bound. I visited my brother and his wife and children on weekends. At Mohammad's, I kept in tenuous contact with the ANM, though the Movement was proscribed and highly disorganized.

We were closer to civilization here, yet worlds apart from the hustle and bustle of Beirut and its intellectual salons and fashionable streets. The people here seemed more mellow, and there was no political life, even of the right-wing variety. For me, it was a period of intellectual incubation and reflection, but not stagnation. There was ample time to study, think, contemplate, and plan.

Most of my colleagues had a hedonistic lifestyle, trying to boost their morale by conspicuously acquiring and consuming more goods. Some sent their parents a fair proportion of their salaries and led an abstemious kind of life. I was politically conscious and a chain smoker—I needed no other diversions.

On January 1, 1965, Fateh opened a new era in modern Palestinian history. This is generally recognized as the date of the modern Palestinian revolution. Armed struggle, long the talk of the salons and work of individuals and small groups, was now translated into action in daily forays into the homeland.

The ANM, of course, had been doing reconnaissance work since 1953 and infiltrating its fedayeen or commandos into occupied Palestine since 1955. The "golden" era of fedayeen activities was in the mid-1950s when the fedayeen used to roam the occupied territories at will. Although the Egyptian government had a role in financing and training the commandos, all missions were conducted by Palestinians who knew the cities and countryside well. Their incursions proved so formidable that Israel used them in 1956 as a pretext to ally with the British and French in the tripartite invasion of Suez.

After the "settlement" of 1957 and withdrawal of foreign troops from Egypt, Nasser banned guerrilla activities, and for eleven years, not a single shot was exchanged across the borders with Israel. Egypt "administered" Gaza behind the UN shield, and the Arab states seemed to act as Israel's sentinels for the next decade, and they too discouraged guerrilla operations.

In the autumn of 1964, activities were revived. The PLO proved to be no panacea; the Arab leaders gradually went back on their liberation pledges. UAR-US relations were deteriorating, and President Johnson was threatening to cut the sales of wheat to Egypt. The Syrian Baathists felt under siege from the UAR and Iraq and encouraged activities that embarrassed Nasser. The Palestinian people were disillusioned with their Arab brethren. All these factors led to a new vitality that surfaced in Palestinian ranks. The climate of opinion favored "doing something."

The key Arab leader, Nasser, was running into difficulties with the United States, which meant he would support the Resistance to bring pressure on Israel and thus improve his bargaining position with America. Nasser usually knew how to manipulate power to his advantage. Interestingly enough, he did not anticipate the impending appearance of Fateh. He must have thought the PLO would be a replica of the fedayeen movement of the mid-fifties.

The new groups that were emerging and eclipsing the PLO were not under Arab League control. The heroes of

Return, Avenging Youth, and Fateh were a different generation of revolutionaries; autonomous groups, not the hirelings of Arab regimes. They expressed the rise of an independent Palestine and asserted the right of Palestinians to self-determination.

At first, Fateh was ignored; later, it was accused of being a Cento agent and even labeled as a right-wing Moslem Brotherhood underground. The more that crimes were attributed to Fateh, the more the Palestinians rallied behind it. The more Fatehites Hussein killed, the more Palestinians joined Fateh. The more bureaucratic and upper-class the PLO became, the more appealing armed struggle became. The new movement provided a spark of hope: armed struggle was the way to salvation. As a Palestinian, I had to believe in the gun as an embodiment of my humanity and my determination to liberate myself and my fellow men. Every self-respecting Palestinian had to become a revolutionary.

The news of revolutionary activity filtered slowly into Kuwait, either by word of mouth, still the most effective means of communication in the Arab world, or by friendly Beiruti or Syrian papers.

The Iraqi, Egyptian, and Jordanian papers reserved their spaces for contemptuous remarks and accusations against "right-wing radicals" who did not see it the Aref-Heikal-Hussein way. With the cessation of American wheat sales to the UAR in 1966, President Nasser started to look upon Fateh more favorably, particularly after Hussein blocked all PLO attempts to organize and station Palestine Liberation Army troops on Jordanian territory.

As Arab leaders repudiated their summit pledges, they began to fall out among themselves, each blaming the other for not carrying out the "resolutions." Nasser supported Fateh because he shared its objectives, not because he was suddenly converted to the cause of people's wars and armed struggle. In this context, Nasser divided the Arab world into progressives and reactionaries, proclaiming himself leader of the progressives.

The Saudis, at the instigation of Washington, decided to propagate the cause of Islam against the "menace of communism," and King Feisal became the leading proponent of the "Islamic pact" designed to include all Islamic states and tie them to Washington.

The Yemeni civil war was concluded in the autumn of 1967 after five years of "revolution." The Yemeni radicals were sacrificed at Khartoum (August 29-September 1) in the name of Arab solidarity and in honor of financial subsidies to Nasser and Hussein from the oil kings. Egypt's fifty thousand troops were withdrawn, and Yemen was abandoned to the winds of conservatism and counterrevolution.

The Palestinian people had spent seventeen years in exile living on hopes fostered by the Arab leadership. In 1965, they decided they must liberate themselves rather than wait for God's help.

Fateh began to occupy a central role in our lives despite its many defects and problems. Its supreme virtue, however, was incontestable: it was a fighting organization in a time when others only talked about the theories of war; it was created by Palestinians to take up armed struggle. Some did. I was not yet ready.

In 1965, my political interests broadened considerably, and thanks to a cowboy from Texas, Lyndon Johnson, I was forced to learn a good deal about Vietnam and Latin America. Next to the Algerians, the Vietnamese were a great source of inspiration to me. Here was a small nation in black pajamas fighting the mightiest empire in world history and defeating it.

As Johnson intensified his bombing attacks, and as his generals promised him victory if only more tons of bombs were dropped on Vietnam, I became angrier and angrier with myself for not being able to do anything to protest or undermine American savagery. The people of Vietnam stood up to the B-52 bombers, though their land was pulverized and practically every square foot of it became a part of an American-made crater. Here was a people with an indomitable spirit, a people whose heroic deeds placed them among the gods; here was a people whose unbound humanity was a blessing to mankind.

The Palestinians must learn the secrets of the Vietnamese: devotion to the cause, sacrifice to the fatherland, absolute commitment to the community; a revolutionary party with a clear conception of ideology, strategy, and organization.

We could do it. We had to do it unless we wished to remain contemptible "refugees."

I hated the American government. And I hated it more when I saw Adlai Stevenson in April of 1965, defending the invasion of the Dominican Republic. I couldn't believe my eyes when I saw the "liberal" hero of the Eisenhower era brandishing the names of "fifty-seven communists" who were members of Colonel Francisco Caamaño's insurgent army.

Twenty thousand U.S. troops were dispatched to Santo Domingo to "safeguard American life and property" – a euphemism that provided a pretext to overthrow the revolutionary government. I almost died laughing when I heard on a BBC broadcast that the Christian Science Monitor checked on the "fifty-seven communists" and found out that most were either dead, in prison, or in exile.

The American troops "liberated" the island, a "free" election was held, and the good people "elected" a lander-aristocratic government led by Mr. Balaguer. All this was done, of course, in loyal homage to liberalism, to the new frontiers, to the good society, and to the American dream.

I understood the direct invasion of Vietnam and the Dominican Republic to be a prelude to the return of the age of gunboat diplomacy, which would soon stretch to the Middle East. I could not predict when the United States or its local power would make a move in our area. It seemed the USA was everywhere on the offensive as the Soviet leadership preached co-existence and tried to practice détente.

From Brazil to Vietnam, from the Dominican Republic to Algeria, from Mali to Indonesia, from Bolivia to Greece, US fleets, air force, and intelligence networks were undermining the achievements of the post-war period and arresting the tide of history.

The 1960s was indeed America's decade. The 1970s shall be the decade of its dismantlement and complete undoing.

The year 1966 was the year of personal mourning for me. Father died after a four-year illness, and I deeply felt the loss of his gentle presence. That autumn, almost every teacher on that staff was wearing black for family losses. All of us were unhappy, and to add to my personal unhappiness, the Kuwaiti government expelled my brother Mohammad for political activities, and Israel started anew its provocative policy of "massive retaliation."

The Zionists were aware of Nasser's weakness and decided to test Arab will by using Fateh's raids on the occupied territory as a pretext to attack Jordan. In November, the Israelis launched a murderous and punishing assault on Es-Samu. The whole town was demolished, and dozens of its inhabitants were killed or injured. The Arab military response was zero. The Arab joint command was a dead letter. The Arabs merely went to the UN and obtained another censure of Israel with America's approval.

A few months later, in April 1967, Syria's "alliance" with Nasser was also tested. On April 7, the Israelis downed Syrian jet fighters while Egyptian Migs looked on, wings folded. The audacious Israelis did not stop there. They knew more than we did. They challenged Nasser in May, and he fell for their trap. In one week in June, the Egyptian army was slaughtered, its armor converted into scrap metal, its "supremacy" in the East was shattered. All the illusions of the Arab nationalists were exploded in two hours and fifty minutes, the time it took the Israeli air force to pulverize the Egyptian air force on the ground on June 5, 1967. A whole era ended; a social class had failed to safeguard Arab interests through stupidity; Arab soldiery lost its moral credibility.

Nasserism, if not Nasser, was dead.

Expecting Arab victory, I refused to believe the outcome. I did believe it when Nasser offered his resignation on June 9, 1967. I awoke from my dream. I smashed my radio and went into a prolonged period of silence. My whole world collapsed. It seemed every Arab had become a slave.

The travel reservations that I had made to return to Palestine to celebrate the recovery of the homeland were canceled. I had no desire to go to Beirut. I felt catatonic for a month, then I decided to go to Lebanon to find out what was happening. My brother Walid brought me up to date on recent developments within the ANM. In the autumn, the Popular Front for the Liberation of Palestine was born.

Here is a summary of the events that occurred in the spring of 1967:

On May 12, 1967, Premier Eshkol and his generals threatened to march to Damascus to topple the Baathist (ruling Social Democratic Party of Syria "hotheads."

On May 14, Soviet and Egyptian intelligence reported a massing of Israeli troops on the Syrian borders. General Amer proposed a pre-emptive attack on the nineteenth anniversary of Israel, but Nasser vetoed him.

On May 17, Nasser ordered the UN emergency forces to withdraw, which they did within two days. On May 18-19, Nasser paraded his battle-dressed troops in front of the Western embassies in Cairo on their way to Sinai.

On May 22, eleven years after the Suez War, Nasser reoccupied Sharm El-Sheikh and declared a blockade of Israeli shipping. Nasser was calling all the shots and dared all enemies. I was elated as the Israelis fumbled, apparently in a state of confusion and irresolution.

On May 26, the ambassadors of the two superpowers, the Soviet and the American, visited Nasser, assuring him that if he did not start the shooting, the Israelis wouldn't. The maritime nations were making noises and plans under United States auspices, but they didn't move. Nasser seemed to be firmly in the saddle.

Hussein rushed to Cairo to pay homage and sign an alliance with Nasser, hoping to cash in on the spoils of war. Nasser called the press of the world and, in one of his last speeches, declared to Israel, "Ahlan Wasahlan, welcome, we are ready, come and fight!"

On June 2, 1967, three days before the Israelis attacked, Nasser was informed by "friends" that the Israelis were going to attack on the morning of June 5. All of us thought that the march to Haifa and Tel Aviv was at most a few weeks' affair. As it turned out, the march to Suez was a six-day endeavor.

Meanwhile, the Israelis struck first, and the UAR eagles never took off the ground; the air force was turned into rubble as the pilots celebrated the birthday of the admiral's daughter, even though an alert had been on for three days.

On June 5, 6, and 7, Radio Cairo and the press announced the shooting down of hundreds of Israeli planes, the capture of cities, and Arab victory! We hailed Arab victory! On the eighth of June, silence prevailed. We knew instantly that something was wrong. At the UN, the UAR accepted a "cease-fire order," and on the ninth, Nasser resigned. The UAR had capitulated; the tide was turned in favor of Israel. The dream ended.

As the protagonists broadcast their war signals from Cairo, Tel Aviv, and other capitals, in Kuwait, we demonstrated in favor of Arab unity and one unified command. I, along with others who had some nursing training, offered to go to the front. We were turned down. Those of us who smoked Western cigarettes suddenly threw them away.

In May, the city of Kuwait truly felt the short spring of the Arab nation. We were overwhelmed by our own illusions when we learned that even little Kuwait was dispatching forces to guard the Arab ramparts and participate in the battle of destiny.

On June 5, the day of reckoning, all teachers went to hospitals to donate blood. For a whole month, I'd been listening to the news on the hour; now was the final hour: was it to be victory or defeat? It was defeat, on a scale much more catastrophic than the Israelis ever dared imagine. Nasser resigned; the masses restored him to power; he lived for three more years.

The summer of 1967 was uneventful. All hope was gone. Little or nothing occurred to rebuild my confidence. I returned to Kuwait with my colleagues. Those whose families were in the West Bank came back with horrifying stories.

The stories had a great impact on each one of us. Details about Zionist atrocities abounded. There were the usual stories of rape, arson, and theft. There were heart-rending accounts of people napalmed from the air, burned to death, or surviving with their whole body scarred. There was a story of a mother who cried to wet the tongue of her dying infant.

The more tales I heard, the more my hatred crystallized. I met a lady from Kalkalia who described to me how that border town was leveled and how other Arab towns were demolished. I listened intently to all the stories. The experience shattered me. Nothing now could avenge Arab honor or liberate the occupied territories; all the diplomatic moves and maneuvers and the summits and the counter-summits and the eloquent speeches did not make one iota of difference. All the work I did for the Red Crescent and the funds I contributed and collected seemed minuscule.

On November 22, the UN Security Council, with Arab approval, sanctified Israel's permanent conquest of my home in Palestine. The UN conferred on Israel the right to use international waterways and the right to recognition with "secure and recognized borders," in return for the settlement of the "refugee problem" and withdrawal to June 4 borders. Israel insisted on total Arab capitulation.

To add to my despair, on October 9, Che Guevara, my hero, was assassinated by CIA-trained Bolivian rangers. The June War shattered my existence, bared my essence. The assassination of Guevara pricked my conscience. Here was an Argentinian radical who had fought beside Fidel Castro in Cuba and helped the revolution attain power on January 1, 1959. His stature in the next eight years assumed international proportions. His personality almost rivaled that of Fidel's. Che sacrificed his personal career as minister of industry when his views and those of Fidel clashed.

Instead of making his differences with Fidel a public issue and undermining the revolution in Cuba, he decided to look for a new homeland for revolutionary action. He toured the African continent and befriended Ben Bella of Algeria and worked in the Congo against the Tshombe secessionist gang and its European mercenaries. Soviet influence eased him out of the Congo.

Finally, he went to Bolivia with a core of sixteen guerrillas, and for eleven months, they struggled to establish a revolutionary base and topple the Barrientos dictatorship. The inhospitability of the terrain, the lack of peasant response, and the opposition of American-trained rangers foredoomed the undertaking. Che nevertheless dared to stand up to America.

His reward was murder on October 9, not by Captain Prado and Colonel Selnich, as the world was led to believe, but by Lyndon Baines Johnson and Hubert Horatio Humphrey. To me, Che's martyrdom can be justified because of its value to world revolution: his life was a form of perpetual renewal; his behavior was exemplary; his commitment was total—qualities the revolutionary movement needed to absorb. His "adventurism and romanticism" are necessary reminders of the unconquerable power of the human spirit in a world where the fear of America cripples millions, deactivates superpowers, and paralyzes professed revolutionaries. Che lived heroically and died heroically.

Yet I, a "revolutionary" woman, was living in tranquility in faraway Kuwait when my people needed revolutionaries and heroes of Che's caliber. I decided I must join the revolution.

PART TWO: The Declaration of a New Humanity – Resistance and Revolution

4 The Road to Haifa

---

Haifa was seized by the Zionists and converted into a European city. It is an extension of Europe's decadence and dehumanization. Haifa cannot be recovered by special prayers to Moshe Dayan. It can only be negated by the birth of a new Palestine, Jewish and Arab.

**Abou Salem**

The Arab masses had, for over a dozen years, pinned their hopes on Nasser to liberate them from Zionism and from their local oppressors. In 1967, after the June tornado, Nasserism lay in shambles.

As Moshe Dayan sat in his office waiting for a telephone call from Cairo expressing Nasser's desire to sign an enduring peace treaty with Israel, the apologists of Nasserism and Baathism were explaining their defeat in terms of "negligence, overconfidence, poor generalship," instead of underlining the real reasons for Israel's stunning victory—decadent Arab social order, corrupt social class, incompetent leadership.

Meanwhile, the Zionists interpreted their victory as a sign of divine grace and choice, the victory of racial superiority and western technology, a proclamation of Sabra morale and social cohesiveness. Yet, for reasons not understood by the imperialist forces, Nasser did not make the expected call to Dayan. He had no desire to capitulate, and had he done so, the Egyptian people would have burned him at the stake. Indeed, no Arab leader, however reactionary, would dare to make peace with Dayan or any other Zionist bully in the future unless he were totally suicidal.

The Palestinian people, however, made a call to Dayan, but it was a call of bombs in broad daylight. The Palestinians had entered the picture as a decisive social force. We decided to make our own history, to speak for ourselves, to seize our own destiny.

No sooner had we arrived on the scene, however, than the Egyptians and Americans, the Israelis and Russians, the Gaullists and Britons, and all the forces of "peace" coalesced and resolved to stamp us out. On the eve of the June War, it appeared to those outside the halls of power that the US and the Soviet Union were on a collision course. To those in the know, however, something very different was happening.

Here is Lester Vellie's inside account from *Countdown in the Holy Land*:

For three years and nine months, the line between the Kremlin and the White House had remained blessedly quiet, carrying only test messages and New Year's Day greetings. Then, on Monday morning, June 5, came the electrifying news that Moscow had activated it seriously for the first time. However, the message was a reassuring one: the Soviet Union would keep hands off the Middle East War, provided the US did the same.

In a cautiously worded reply, Johnson agreed. Mr. Johnson's "cautiously worded reply" was a simple way of keeping his options flexible. He was assured by his CIA, Pentagon, and State Department officers that Israel would win within four days.

Had these calculations gone wrong, however, there was no doubt that the US would have intervened. According to Vellie, whose source is the State Department and Pentagon, it was morally and practically "inconceivable" that the US would not intervene: Israel is one of the few democracies in all of Asia and the Middle East. Since the world regards the US as Israel's protector, whether the US wishes to be or not, Israel's destruction, with Soviet help, while the US stood idly by, would send tremors of fear throughout the non-communist world. Further, if Israel went down, no other pro-Western nations in the Middle East would be safe from Nasser and the Russians.

If the decision of the two superpowers "not to intervene" had been taken on June 5, and they seemed to be on a collusion rather than a collision course, what then was the value of that verbal combat at the UN, and why was the Special Emergency Session of the General Assembly called by the Soviet Union? The verbal exchange at the UN had only a psychological impact as both powers resumed rearming their respective clients instantaneously.

On June 19, 1967, Kosygin, leading a high-powered Soviet delegation at the UN, condemned Israel as an aggressor, demanded that Israel withdraw to the June 4 borders, and urged the UN to make Israel pay reparations for damages inflicted on the Arabs.

One hour before Kosygin delivered his speech, President Johnson outlined the American position on the Middle East before the National Foreign Policy Conference for Educators in Washington. Here are the "five great principles" of peace which were, in effect, the substantive points of the Eban rebuttal to Mr. Kosygin's speech at the UN:

1. **The right to life of all the nations in the area**
2. **Justice for the refugee**
3. **Respect for maritime rights**
4. **Filing of reports by all UN member nations on their arms shipments to the Middle East**
5. **Respect for political independence and territorial integrity based on peace**
    - The last point also advised "adequate recognition of the special interests of three great religions in the holy places of Jerusalem."

I am certain that if a comparison were made between what Johnson said in Washington and what Eban said at the UN, it would reveal systematic collaboration between their coterie of writers, if not collective authorship of the two speeches.

Be that as it may, however, the crucial point to remember here is that the speeches of both reflected the viewpoint of the victor. It is obvious why most of the dwarf states at the UN—African, Latin, and Asian—thought that Johnson and Eban were reasonable, impartial, and indeed magnanimous in victory. Since the Soviets were on the side of the vanquished and had substituted propaganda for collective action with the Arabs, there was no other course of action they could adopt.

Both participants and spectators refused to take note of the following:

1. All UN spokesmen who purported to speak for Palestine denied the Palestinians' peoplehood and classified the Palestinians as refugees.
2. They all regarded the conflict as being Arab governments versus a Jewish state, as opposed to the conception of the conflict as being Arab versus Zionist and oppressed versus imperialist oppressors.
3. They all prescribed some kind of regional political solution between existing political entities, instead of envisaging the creation of a new social order where Arab and Jew could be self-determining within the framework of a unified Arab socialist republic.

Therefore, by definition, all states proposed solutions that had to be rejected by the Palestinians with alarm. Every solution that presupposed the continued existence of the Zionist state in our midst was antithetical to the Arab social revolution.

The deafening verbal blasts at the UN only concealed the political chicanery. The vanquished accepted a cease-fire on the basis of the accomplished military conquest. The

UN passed no resolution demanding Israeli withdrawal. It merely established observer groups on both sides of the Suez Canal, and the Israelis settled down to building Nabals (paramilitary colonies) and kibbutzim all over the area referred to firstly as "conquered," then "administered zones," and now "liberated" territories.

The Soviets and Americans returned to the regular autumn session of the General Assembly and delivered more bombast, reiterated their previous positions, and presented the same resolutions. The Arab diplomats talked as if they were the conquerors and demanded complete Israeli withdrawal. They invoked the principles of Western morality and justice, not realizing that those very principles were the ones used to justify Zionist "humanity" towards the Arabs.

Finally, with the agreement or acquiescence of all concerned, the UN Security Council unanimously passed its famous British (242) resolution on November 22, 1967. Here is the preamble and the operative paragraphs of the resolution:

---

### The Security Council,

Expressing its continuing concern with the grave situation in the Middle East, emphasizing the inadmissibility of the acquisition of territory by war and the need to work for a just and lasting peace in which every state in that area can live in security, emphasizing further that all member states in their acceptance of the Charter of the United Nations have undertaken a commitment to act in accordance with Article 2 of the Charter.

**I. Affirms that the fulfillment of Charter principles requires the establishment of a just and lasting peace in the Middle East, which should include the application of both the following principles:**

1. Withdrawal of Israeli armed forces from territories of recent conflict.
2. Termination of all claims or states of belligerency and respect for and acknowledgment of the sovereignty, territorial integrity, and political independence of every state in the area and their right to live in peace within secure and recognized boundaries free from threats or acts of force.
3. Affirms further the necessity for guaranteeing freedom of navigation through international waterways in the area.
4. For achieving a just settlement of the refugee problem.
5. For guaranteeing the territorial inviolability and political independence of every state in the area, through measures including the establishment of demilitarized zones.
6. Requests the Secretary-General to designate a special representative to proceed to the Middle East to establish and maintain contacts with the states concerned in order to promote agreement and assist efforts to achieve a peaceful and accepted settlement in accordance with the provisions and principles in this resolution.

7. Requests the Secretary-General to report to the Security Council on the progress of the efforts of the special representative as soon as possible.

Resolution 242 obviously embodies the points proclaimed by Mr. Johnson in his speech of June 19 and includes the Soviet-Arab demand of Israeli withdrawal without specification or insistence on total and immediate withdrawal.

More importantly, however, while the resolution refers to the "inadmissibility" of the acquisition of territory by war, it ipso facto sanctions Israel's conquest by offering to trade her conquest for "secure and recognized boundaries" and by conferring on Israel all the legitimate attributes of permanent and unchallenged statehood.

Lastly, the resolution paternalistically alludes to a "just settlement of the refugee problem," as if we were some kind of environmental pollution that had to be grappled with, while the "territorial inviolability and political independence of every state in the area" are upheld and guaranteed.

Western diplomats claimed that Resolution 242 represented "a solid gain for Western diplomacy," and a serious reversal for the Soviet Union's Middle East policy. In an anti-climactic speech on November 23, 1967, President Nasser gave his response to the infamous Resolution 242.

Nasser enumerated Egypt's war losses and disclosed that eighty percent of its military equipment was destroyed; that over 100,000 soldiers and 1,500 officers were killed and more than 5,500 men were taken prisoner. Then, with all the strength he could muster, Nasser declared that he was stronger in November than he was in May of 1967.

But his ambivalent but weak position was revealed by his implicit acceptance of 242, and he could merely argue that 242 was "insufficient and unclear."

The atmosphere at this time was bleak for me. I was uncertain and despondent. In the autumn, I returned to Kuwait and compared notes with my colleagues.

Those who had been in the occupied territories were indignant and talked about the possibilities of armed struggle; those who had visited elsewhere in the Arab world came back angered, frustrated, confused, and dismayed. Nothing changed the atmosphere drastically that autumn.

With the approach of the new year, news of renewed Fateh activity was filtering into Kuwait. I was told in a hushed tone by a friend that the Popular Front for the Liberation of Palestine (PFLP) had been proclaimed in November. However, no other concrete information reached us regarding the PFLP.

While I was in Lebanon during the summer, I was unable to make any direct contacts with my former associates outside of Sour. For a whole academic year, I was unaware of PFLP developments. Since the open ANM cells had been eliminated in 1965-66 in Kuwait, there was less opportunity to convert the ANM branch into PFLP cells, although the transformation was being carried out in other parts of the Arab world. There was nothing else to do but to try and participate in Fateh activities. I did.

At the outset, most of the teachers who were politically inclined had no clear idea of what action to take. Nothing was happening as we settled into another monotonous year of teaching. We continued, as usual, our campaign of indoctrinating the students and discussing how Nasserism failed to unify and defend the Arab world. We focused on this point as a defensive posture against attacks on the Palestinians for causing the Egyptian debacle.

It seemed then that the general public sympathized with President Nasser and felt that the easiest way of silencing the Palestinians was to use them as scapegoats. My colleagues and I didn't feel guilty; we merely went on the defensive. Later, we used the attacks as starting points to criticize not Nasser but Nasserism.

Fateh was the only revolutionary organization whose activities were tolerated in Kuwait. The PLO, although recognized as a legal Palestinian entity by the government, had neither leaders nor followers of any significant number. I myself had outgrown my original lukewarm sympathies for it and sought another outlet for my political energies. Fateh, having renewed its military operations on August 18, 1967, presented an opportunity and a challenge.

Along with our principal and a handful of tears, I endeavored to work through Fateh to liberate Palestine. I had been raised in the good ANM tradition of question and debate. For every project we undertook, for every action we contemplated, for every view we held, the

ANM had offered a rationale, a way of ascertaining and examining the facts, an opportunity to propose alternative programs. Fateh was something new in my experience. Our sole function was fundraising.

We were not a part of the policy-making processes but merely spectators or ticket agents in the temple of Fateh. Periodically, nebulous lectures were given; speakers always remained within the realm of glittering generalities in dealing with the strategy, ideology, financing, and recruiting of the movement.

Initially, I thought it was impertinent on my part to ask too many questions since I was a novice in Fateh's ranks. Then I decided that I, as a Palestinian, should know what we were doing to create a new Palestine. I began pressing for answers:

- To whom was the movement accountable?
- Why had it accepted funds from Saudi Arabia and other reactionary sources?
- What was the nature of Fateh's socio-economic program?
- Why had Fateh tried to isolate itself from the Arab masses?
- More importantly, I wanted to know what women could do beyond fundraising.

Most of the answers were not forthcoming, and those that were were extremely inadequate. We were told that the movement was autonomous and its leaders must remain anonymous for security reasons. Fateh, as I learned later, was the most open secret in the world, where the pseudonyms and the real names of the leaders were known to the whole world, and the movement acted and operated in the open in Amman before the eyes of friends and foes.

As to why funds were accepted from Saudi Arabia, my education commissar informed me that in the liberation stage, we must ally ourselves even with the devil in order to win. He insisted that only the Palestinians should be allowed to participate in the revolution.

At that time, Fateh did not recruit or accept Arab recruits in its ranks, but later slightly modified the rule under pressure, as if the Arabs were a different race of people. Abu Ali was not convincing; he only increased my doubts. Yet, I continued to work through Fateh because I had no alternative. He often asked me why I was so troublesome and asked so many embarrassing questions. I always said:

"Abu Ali, we can't win unless we have a reasonably clear program and organized members. Besides, we must know the whole truth regarding the revolution, not only its slogans."

By posing questions, I triggered off a chain of events that higher officials had to deal with. Friends and supporters of the movement were growing uneasy because the relationship with Fateh was solely material, not a relationship sustained by political interaction or participation in the political process. My message was getting through to my audience. I asked questions in a restrained manner and was too well known and too generous a contributor to be dismissed as an unfriendly critic. Fateh had to provide the answers.

A prominent person came to see me, Fathi Arafat, brother of Yassir, the leader of Fateh. We had a long talk and exchanged ideas. The most important point I raised was the question of women and their role in Fateh. I pleaded with him to let me join their military wing, Al-Assifah, because I had been militarily trained for years. I was prepared to go on patrols and operations inside the occupied territories. He promised to see what he could do and report back to me.

A month later, Fathi asked me if I could go to Al Aghwar on the Jordanian side of the River Jordan. I enthusiastically said yes and made plans. To this day, he has not returned to tell me when and where to report or whom to contact.

Meanwhile, my fellow Fatehites in Kuwait were kind enough to find a role for me. They proposed that a group of us do something creative for the summer of 1968. They suggested we could perform two important tasks—assisting overworked mothers in the "refugee" camps and visiting the families of our martyrs.

"Social work," I scoffed, "is not social revolution. I want to participate fully in the revolution." Such talk was eclipsed on March.

21, when Fateh scored a historic first and the tide of Arab despondency began to ebb. It was the Battle of Karameh, March 21, 1968, the making and undoing of Fateh.

Karameh was a Palestinian city on the east side of the River Jordan, created out of nothing by the Palestinians after 1948. It was a symbol of hope and dignity.

The Israelis tried to obliterate Karameh and failed, for the first time in their long string of military victories. They were trounced in a psychological sense, but victorious if we measure the operation in strict military terms.

It was a turning point, and the Arab news media inflated the incident to make it appear as if the liberation of Palestine was just around the corner. Thousands of volunteers poured in; gold was collected in kilos, arms came by the ton.

Fateh, a movement of a few hundred semi-trained guerrillas, suddenly appeared to the Arabs like the Chinese liberation army on the eve of October 1949. Even King Hussein declared that he was a commando!

The Arab Palestinian masses felt that in a few months, Palestine was going to be recovered. The euphoric atmosphere gathered momentum as the Arab governments joined the chorus of Fateh adherents, supplying it with rockets, military transport, artillery, etc. They made the revolution affluent. The Arab governments needed Fateh as a shield to cover up their own incompetence.

Fateh became a folk song, a fashion, a fetish. Its leaders, cadres, and office clerks were regarded as saviors, saints, and seraphims. Fateh, with Yassir Arafat as its chairman, was flirting with the PLO.

In July 1968, while Fateh and the PLO were playing hide-and-seek and enjoying the comfort of the Nile Hilton, three lonely revolutionaries performed a dramatic history-making feat, which the new PLO denounced.

The Popular Front for the Liberation of Palestine seized an El-Al aeroplane of the Israeli semi-military, semi-civilian airlines. The aircraft was taken to the Arab state of Algeria, and the latter released the plane and passengers without insisting on exchanging them.

Israel, the world Zionist conclave, the imperialists, the Arab states, and the PLO and Co. all assailed the PFLP and accused it of air piracy. All of a sudden, Israel was able to count friends in "progressive" Arab circles.

The incident was an eye-opener for me. It was the beginning of the end of my exile. I was about to be liberated; I had found an alternative to Fateh, and I sought to make contacts with the PFLP.

At about the same time, in a seemingly insignificant event, a YWCA American girl, Jane Marlowe, came to live at our house in Sour for a week. She was placed in our home because my younger sister Khaledia had some relations with the YWCA and because most of us spoke English at home.

Jane was a typical Yankee do-gooder who came to Sour to teach the "refugees" swimming, drawing, fun, and games. Like most American missionaries who come to the Arab world—whatever the garb they wear— Jane was a "pacifist" who advocated peace among the Semitic brothers, believing there was plenty of room for all in the region.

We tried to tell her that the issue was not only territory but also imperialism and Zionism, and whether the Arab and Jewish masses would determine their future for themselves or allow the vampires of American and

Zionist high finance to determine it for them. Jane told us that the word "vampire" was hyperbole and lectured us on the necessity of using analytical language rather than emotion-laden slogans. She was not as perceptive and well-informed as she claimed, and in a few minutes, we discovered where her real, liberal sympathies lay.

She referred to Fateh as a terrorist organization that deliberately mined roads and killed Israeli schoolchildren. She showed how color-blind and profound she was by telling us that the Palestinians should live among their brothers in the Arab states and avoid being discriminated against in Israel. We smiled sardonically as Jane revealed her ignorance of the plight of the Palestinians. She was blissfully unaware that she was spouting the Zionist line about the Palestinian problem and advocating the "final solution" that the Zionists proposed for our eternal peace. Jane had read her New York Times well and pontificated "objectively" on the need for "peace and stability" in the area. She was a Catholic girl from the Bronx who knew what was good for Arabs and Jews.

We heatedly debated both sides of the "Arab-Israeli conflict," the morality of hijacking, and the legitimacy of revolutionary violence. She was aware of the Phantoms her government supplied to Israel to maintain "the balance of power" in the Middle East, and she was opposed to the Zionist privilege of collecting tax-free dollars from America. But she saw all these things in terms of "the arms race" and Russia's expansionist policies.

She did concede the right of the oppressed to take up arms against their oppressors and saw the political value of hijacking, if not the morality. I explained to her that the Israelis held thousands of Arab prisoners and threatened the lives of Palestinians daily. If she wanted to be impartially ethical, she must pass moral judgments on the Israelis, not on us, because our actions were merely sporadic responses to a tyrannical social system.

Although she remained "liberal" in her attitude, she posed some poignant questions that had a lasting impact on me.

"Are you a refugee, Leila?" she said to me.

"Technically, yes; emotionally, no," I replied. "I am no longer a refugee because I am a revolutionary."

She looked around her and surveyed our apartment building, then pointedly asked, "Do you expect to live in Palestine more luxuriously than you are living here, if and when you get there?"

"Perhaps not, but that is not important," I answered.

"It is very important," she insisted, "because you wouldn't give up what you have here, and you're not doing anything personally to reach your goals."

Jane stunned me. My mind went blank. I thought for a minute and admitted, "Jane, you are right. I am only talking. I haven't done anything concrete."

To calm myself, I went to the veranda, looked longingly southward to the mountains beyond in Palestine, and secretly promised to join in the struggle of my people. Jane was feeling triumphant as I returned inside. I spoke sorrowfully, "The Palestinians are a hardworking people, but they are a dissipated people; a good many have educated themselves well, but so few, including the Khaled family, are doing anything to express their collective existence as a people." I looked at my younger brothers, who had angrily attacked Jane for criticizing the El-Al hijack and for being a Zionist. I said in English,

"The lady from America has been a good teacher. She has forced us to recognize and think about our obligations to our people. We ought not to be angry with her but thank her for helping us expose ourselves to ourselves. We must act, not just talk and memorize the arguments against Zionism." My brothers, ashamed, withdrew from the room. Jane and I sat down for a heart-to-heart talk. Before and during my association with Fateh, I had misgivings about its political and ideological attitudes, but it was the foreign operations of the PFLP as well as Fateh's embrace of the PLO that made me realize that Fateh was not the best Palestinian response to its enemies.

I was finally convinced when I heard heroic tales of the PFLP underground from my fellow teachers who had been in the occupied territories. I resolved that I must join the PFLP. The problem was how to contact their underground in Kuwait.

One day it happened by accident. I was passing by the South Arabian Bookstore where a man was selling PFLP Christmas cards. I looked carefully at his cards, all the while trying to determine whether or not he was a member of the PFLP or just a friend. He wouldn't comment himself. I pleaded, "I want to get in touch with the PFLP very badly, and I want to join; believe me, I want to join. I am a Palestinian, I want to fight, I want to go to the occupied territories. Please tell me whom to see or contact. Surely if you are a supporter of the PF, you'll help me." He listened to my plea and told me to return the following Thursday afternoon between three and four, and he'd introduce me to the local representative. I was overjoyed. I arrived two hours before the appointed time and waited inside the Bookstore, leafing through journals, pamphlets, and books of the Arab and international left. Precisely at three, a tall, handsome young man walked into the Bookstore. He looked very solemn as he greeted the cards "salesman." I presumed he was the PF man. I introduced myself. He was reserved and courteous. I told him who I was and said I was anxious to join their military underground. He gave me a comradely pat on the shoulders and said:

"I regret to inform you, Leila, that you have to be educated first."

"Educated?" I said as I drew away. "I am a teacher and I know how to read and write and all that."

"No, Leila, I didn't mean educated in that sense," Abu Nidal said. "You'll have to study the ideology and strategy of the PFLP and work with the other comrades first; then we will decide where your talents could best be put in the service of the revolution."

I interrupted. "I want to fight; I can't wait, and what do I need such a fancy language for anyway?"

Patiently, Abu Nidal explained: "Leila, the liberation of Palestine is going to be a long, long struggle. You will have ample time to prove your prowess. Believe me, if you're capable of fighting and wish to fight, the PF will not hesitate to send you anywhere you're needed."

I was cheered by his reassuring promise, but I wanted to make sure that I was not going to be left stranded. "What should I do then?" I asked.

"First of all," he said, "you will have to spread the word at your place of work and form a study group to educate yourselves and undertake various projects to help the PF financially. Next week we will meet here again and continue our discussion. We will get in touch with you if you forget to get in touch with us." I left the bookstore and went home at peace with myself. I felt I was on the road to Haifa. I was coming out of the abyss.

The same evening, I contacted some of my close friends. We spent the whole night together evaluating the political affiliation and commitment of each teacher. We decided that we had a large number of sympathizers and could probably form a cell in a few weeks.

From now on, we met regularly every week, and I saw Abu Nidal periodically to obtain PF literature and advice. Abu Nidal also put me in touch with some former comrades from the old ANM who had joined the PF. We were slowly building a PF network in Kuwait. The assault on the El-Al plane on December 26, 1968, in Athens gave us a big push, especially after December 28, when the Israelis raided Beirut International Airport and destroyed thirteen Middle East Airlines planes. We thanked the Israelis for enlisting Lebanese support for the revolution and admired their audacity in blowing up planes that were seventy to eighty percent American-owned. From our vantage point, we were anxious to see the consequences. The world was at last forced to take notice of Palestinian actions.

The Arab press couldn't ignore them, nor could the Zionists conceal them. The Israelis had helped the cause more than we dared contemplate by their prompt and decisive "reprisal." It seemed the more spectacular the action, the better the morale of our people. We looked forward to more.

Here is the aim of the Palestine revolution as spelled out in the PF program.

The Palestinian liberation movement is not racist or hostile to the Jews. It is not aimed at the Jewish people. Its aim is to break the Israeli military, political, and economic entity, which is based on aggression, expansion, and organic unity with the interests of imperialism in our homeland. It is against Zionism as a racist, aggressive movement in alliance with imperialism. Zionism has capitalized on the suffering of the Jewish people to serve its interests and those of imperialism in this rich part of the world, which is the gateway to the countries of Africa and Asia. The aim of the Palestinian liberation movement is the establishment of a national democratic state in Palestine in which the Arabs and Jews can live as equal citizens with regard to rights and duties, forming an integral part of the democratic, progressive Arab national existence, which will live peacefully with all the progressive forces in the world.

The Palestinian liberation movement is a progressive national movement against the forces of aggression and imperialism. The link between the interests of imperialism and the continued existence of Israel will make our war against the latter basically a war against imperialism. On the other hand, the link between the Palestinian liberation movement and the Arab progressive movement will make our war against Israel that of 100 million Arabs in their national and unified struggle. The battle of Palestine today, and all the objective circumstances surrounding it, will make the war a starting point for the attainment of the interconnected aims of the Arab revolution.

Lastly, the Palestinian war, as far as the Palestinian and Arab people are concerned, will lead to the civilization of the Arabs and result in the transition of the Arab people from the state of under-development to the requirements of modern life. Through our war of liberation, we shall acquire political awareness of the facts of this age, and we shall throw aside delusions and learn the value of facts.

The habits of under-development exemplified in surrender, dependence, individuality, tribalism, laziness, anarchy, and extemporization will be changed through the war of liberation. In their place will come: the realization of the value of time, organization, accuracy, objective thinking, the importance of collective action, planning, total mobilization; interest in education and acquisition of all its weapons, and knowledge of the value of the human being; the freeing of woman—half of society—from the bondage of decadent habits and customs; the basis of nationalism in confronting dangers and the supremacy of this connection over tribalism and regionalism.

Our long-term national war of liberation implies our fusion in a new way of life and our starting point on the road of progress and civilization.

The enemy camp is defined as follows:

1. The enemy of the Arabs in the war of liberation is Israel, Zionism, world imperialism, and Arab reaction.
2. This enemy has definite technological superiority which naturally is converted to military superiority and a great fighting force.
3. The enemy has long experience in opposing the people's development towards economic and political liberation. It has the ability to abort revolutions.
4. The nature of the war of liberation, as far as the main military base of this enemy—Israel—is concerned, is a war of life or death which the political and military leadership inside Israel will attempt to fight until the last breath. The National Front and the forces that constitute the revolution: We consider Palestinian national unity as essential in the mobilization of all the forces of the revolution to resist the enemy camp. On this basis, we should adopt a definite stand in this direction.
5. The form of national unity is the creation of a front in which all the classes of the revolution—workers, peasants, and petit bourgeoisie—should be represented.

We should attend actively to the mobilization of workers and peasants in one revolutionary political organization armed with the ideology of scientific socialism. On this basis, we should actively attempt to unify all the left-wing Palestinian organizations which, through dialogue between them and through their experience, can commit themselves to such an analysis.

The petit bourgeoisie will not join an organization committed to scientific socialism and strong political organization. Thus, it will join those Palestinian organizations which raise general liberal slogans, avoid clarity in thinking and analysis of class structure, and exist in an organizational form that does not require of the petit bourgeoisie more than its capacity. In other words, the petit bourgeoisie will fill, in the first place, the ranks of El-Fateh and the Palestine Liberation Organization (PLO).

On this basis, and on the basis of our understanding of the basic conflict, the nature of the present phase, and the necessity of national unity to assemble all the forces of the revolution to resist Israel, we should work for the establishment of a national front with El-Fateh and the PLO which can offer the war of liberation the necessary class alliance on the one hand, and protect the right of each class to view the war and plan for it in accordance with its class vision on the other.

Our study group was rapidly mastering the strategy and ideology of the PF and moving towards the cell stage. On the advice of Abu Nidal, we were studying more advanced radical books and broadening our horizons when another Palestinian woman revolutionary made world headlines and shook our movement. The morning of February 18 was just another day for me. As usual, I got up at five-thirty a.m. to prepare breakfast and listen to the BBC news. Suddenly, I heard over the air the name of Amina Dhahbour. She had been in on an attack on an El-Al plane in Zurich. She was the first woman to participate in a foreign operation. The news struck me like lightning. A Palestinian woman, a revolutionary, in the citadel of financial capitalism! Fortunately, the BBC announcers regularly repeat the major news items and read them over in detail, for I wasn't certain at first whether I was hearing or imagining.

I ran out in my pajamas, screaming throughout the dormitory. "She did it! She did it! Palestine will be free!" Everyone thought that I had gone mad. But I made sure that everyone got the message: A Palestinian woman was fighting while we were talking in far-away Kuwait. Within a few minutes, we were all celebrating the liberation of Palestine and the liberation of women. Fateh and PF women embraced and danced the Palestine Debke together in the corridors of El-Shaab. The PFLP had earned its way to the El-Shaab teaching staff and their wallets. We decided that henceforth, all funds collected must be distributed equally between Fateh and the PF. The Fateh sisters acquiesced; they had no choice. The school became a beehive for the resistance. Even the pupils were turned into revolutionary salesmen and fundraisers.

We indoctrinated them so well that some of them turned out to be more effective supporters of the resistance than many of us.

That same day, I called comrade Abu Nidal and informed him that I wanted to join the Special Operations Squad. He agreed. From then on, I received advanced, highly specialized training. It was now only a matter of time until I participated in a foreign military operation. The hour of reckoning was drawing closer for me.

While I engaged in intensive training, I continued teaching and converted my study group into a tradition-breaking cell. In Kuwait, politics were forbidden, but six women decided to stake their careers and reputation in the name of resistance. On an April morning, the Muslim Easter, we marched to the center of Kuwait carrying PF collection boxes and requesting donations. At first, the other women were not enthusiastic; they were frightened. I was shameless and fearless; nothing mattered to me but the revolution. We quickly discovered that the people were more advanced than we thought. They not only contributed generously but urged us to mobilize others to help canvas the whole city, which we did. The women joined the vanguard. The masses filled our coffers. No one, not even official sources, criticized our action. Kuwait City was ready to join the move to social progress.

Encouraged by this response, I decided to earn some money for the PF by tutoring in English and by using the talent for hairdressing that I had acquired in Lebanon as a youngster. Without revealing details of my political affiliation, I applied for and got a job in a beauty salon for the two-week Easter vacation. After hours, I worked tirelessly to raise funds for the PF. I seized every opportunity to propagate the cause. One day, an affluent-looking lady who must have been pleased by the hairstyle I gave her, gave me a twenty-five fils tip. I hesitated for a moment, then accepted it and gave her a receipt for it. The lady was surprised when she saw the stamp of the Popular Front on it.

But she gave me another dinar and wished the PF well. My employer, who had witnessed the exchange, was not angry. She said that she sympathized with the cause, but she asked me to keep my politics to myself. I was especially careful and courteous in dealing with people, and she said such revolutionary qualities were necessary for Arab women. When I left, she gave me my pay plus a five dinar donation to the PF.

The PF was indeed making friends.

I was not, however, the happiest of women. The party was making me do this sort of work that I didn't enjoy. I was restless for action. That spring, I said goodbye to teaching and to my Kuwaiti friends: my time had come. I headed for Amman. My Russian-made gun, the Semenov, became my companion!

When I arrived in Amman, the city was swarming with guerrillas. It felt good to be a Palestinian in one's homeland. Within a few days, with twenty women comrades, I was taken to a military camp north of Amman where we were to undergo more intensive and specialized training. Here I met the legendary heroine of our underground in the occupied territory, Rashida Obeida.

She was a truly impressive human being as well as a beautiful woman. She knew how to handle a gun, and she knew when to use it for the cause. I made friends with her and Feihaa Abdul El-Hadi almost immediately.

Before we embarked on a mission to test our endurance, the head of the military school, comrade Hassan, gave us a final briefing in which he distinguished between mere political agitation and fundraising and politico-military work. He concluded his speech by saying, "This phase of our work is harsh and severe. Once you start it, you can't withdraw until the objective is accomplished.

Therefore," he continued, "examine your consciences, comrades, and see if you're really up to it—if not, please depart in peace." Startled, we each looked around and wondered whether we should proceed or withdraw. A three-hour "struggle session" followed. The arguments centered around whether our training was going to be used or whether we were just training for contingencies. We also argued about individuality, the role of women in the Movement, and the kind of relationship we were going to have with parents, boyfriends, or husbands. If a woman decided to commit herself to

this phase of the revolution, it meant the final break with her past and relegating her private life and desires to a secondary position. If she was unable to accept these terms, then she could make a partial commitment to become a supporter or a friend of the resistance rather than train to become a professional revolutionary. Those who chose the military option were to remain for further training.

The women who thought of the training period as a pleasant summer promenade began to retreat. Rashida and I immediately upbraided the comrade who pointed out that she had no formal permission from her parents to be in the camp.

Rashida told her bluntly:

"Sister, if at twenty-five you still have to depend on your mother's approval, you do not belong in the Popular Front. You should go back home and ask your mother to find you a husband and

prepare an attractive dowry for you."

I was less harsh than Rashida. "Look, sisters, Palestine beckons us to redeem her, and here we are squabbling among ourselves about parents and families. I think we should overcome this kind of adolescence and act as grown-up women, not as appendages to our men or maids to our parents." I looked Salwa in the eye and said, "If you wish to leave, no one will stop you. If you're incapable of acting as a mature and self-determining woman, return home for further

`training.'"

In the heat of the debate, three women collapsed under the pressure and decided they didn't belong in this phase of the work. Comrade Hassan re-entered the tent as the sunshine patriots departed. He wished them well. The rest of us hurried to make plans for survival in the arid mountains of Jordan. Night was settling in.

The plains and the cities below were our guardians. I was tense and didn't sleep well that night. Most of us were very on edge for the next few days. Some had misgivings, others feared the unknown. I realized that at last my dream was coming true and overcame my tenseness. I had no time for prolonged doubt or fright. I had lived that agonizing period months before. I was ready for action.

Action was forthcoming, but not in the expected form. On the third night of our stay in the mountains, a comrade guard was nervously watching for Zionist infiltrators and walking gingerly when she heard a strange sound. She ordered the infiltrator to stop and identify himself. He didn't.

She fired into the darkness. In seconds, everyone in the camp was crawling on their stomachs in search of the enemy. Soulafah continued firing as we zeroed in on the target, knowing that if she killed one intruder, at least two or three others must be at large in the vicinity. We quickly found out that there were none and that the comrade guard had indeed scored: she had killed a donkey invader! We had a brief meeting and decided to pay the owners of the donkey the required price, but no one ever claimed the poor wandering beast.

A few days after the donkey affair, there were no jokes. Our intelligence relayed a message that the Israelis were planning to bomb our camp at five a.m. on June 5, to celebrate the second anniversary of the June War. At three a.m. I had just returned from maneuvers and wanted to catch an hour or two of sleep. But Comrade Bassim ordered us to depart immediately and made preparations to move out heavy equipment. It so happened that we were being visited that evening by a group of Iraqi artists who wanted to live the revolution and witness the work of revolutionaries.

The comrade artists had their fill that night as they joined our column's march in darkness. At the appointed time, the Israeli bombers swooped over the area, dropped their flares and bombs without being challenged, and turned the early morning sunshine into a blinding column of smoke. They strafed the whole region for several minutes with their hell of iron and destruction and then returned home safely. We were helpless. Hussein's air force was on the ground; it was not intended for use against the Israelis but against the Palestinians who didn't own a single civilian plane. The world's press reported the incident as Israeli reconnaissance and termed the second anniversary of the June War "peaceful." We returned to camp, rebuilt it in a few days, and resumed our preparations to confront the Zionist enemy.

At camp, I did my utmost to prove that I was fit to be a good guerrilla fighter. I carried out orders conscientiously. My instructors offered no criticism, expressed no admiration, and had no particular plan for me. I knew that the PF leadership would take my personal desires into consideration but would decide what missions I was to undertake on the basis of my potential and performance.

The training schedule was exacting but occasionally left us time for a little fun. We were "entertaining" a group of foreign students and trying to lead a Bedouin kind of life in order to politicize our Bedouin population. The students had been attending an international solidarity meeting in Amman held under the auspices of the General Union of Palestinian Students. Most were graduates of the 1968 university upheavals in the West. We found it very amusing that they honestly believed they were making a

"Revolution" if they undressed in public, seized a university building, or shouted an obscenity at bureaucrats. I was initially opposed and refused to talk to them, even though some believed in violent revolution, because I didn't want to be another experimental

"guinea pig" to Westerners. I finally relented and

I am glad I did. I hadn't met Western

"revolutionaries" before. It turned out they represented an unfamiliar cultural rather than a political phenomenon.

Some seemed to have read the historic political literature of the left, but most regarded the Marxist-Leninist leaders disdainfully, with the exception of the "Young Marx," who held some sort of fascination for a few of them.

Though we were impressed by their moral integrity and personal dedication, we felt their ideology and strategy had little to do with the making of revolution. Some Americans were quite serious and believed in the historic mission of the working class and were making plans to integrate themselves with the masses. What astonished us most about this group was that they were opposed to nationalism, a doctrine we hold dearly as a colonized and dissipated people. Some believed in violence for "the hell of it" and in students as revolutionary agents of history. But the majority were inclined towards guerrilla theatre as a means of "making revolution." They performed a little for us.

As they were departing, I was rather struck by a French anarchist student who proclaimed, "Let chaos reign," and by a German who echoed the same sentiment. I exclaimed that the Palestinian people were an example of a society in chaos without authority and leadership, which, as a result, was left at the mercy of the Zionist oppressor. I asked them what could they prescribe for us in order to overcome our kind of "alienation"—beards, long hair, and toy guns?

They merely paused, they smiled, they reflected, they inhaled, and passed their joints on in universal wonder.

One of the most serious problems the resistance has experienced, and one that it has failed to face, is the integration of the Palestinian and Jordanian masses. Fateh made no genuine effort to reach the people in Jordan. We in the Front believed not only in Arab unity in general but also in the indissolubility of the Jordanian and Palestinian people. Hence, we worked with the Bedouin population near our camp, and we were able to win them over to the side of the revolution. We even trained a large number of them in the art of espionage and offered them ideological as well as military training. Our open and friendly relations with them enabled some of us to visit their tents and give talks to whole families and sometimes even whole tribes.

I, along with our squad commander, Bassim, was a frequent visitor, and occasionally we were invited as guests to their feasts. I remember vividly the night we attended a wedding dinner celebrated before the parents of the bride took their daughter to the groom's tent. A desert moon whispered love to those assembled; it was a night to love and be loved. Gracious maidens danced, their flowing rainbow-colored robes touching our cheeks gently. All was joy; all was fun.

Bassim and I were beginning to fall in love. But before we could share in the pleasure of the occasion, a messenger suddenly rushed in and handed me a two-word note: return immediately. I leapt to my feet, wished the bride well, and returned hurriedly to camp. The commander was curt. "We received an order saying you should be in Beirut tomorrow at ten a.m. It is now 9 p.m."

I immediately packed my belongings and headed to Amman and out to Beirut, not knowing what was in the offing for me. There were some complications on the border with Syria, but they were settled, and I reached Beirut in time. The comrade who was waiting for me looked casual and friendly as I stormed in, spouting indignant protests, "I told you that I make my own decisions. I don't want to leave the Front now after all that training and hard work."

He was puzzled for a moment. "I know that; that is why I sent for you. Why are you shouting?"

I apologized. "I thought you were going to release me under pressure from the family." He smiled reassuringly, then his tone became very serious, "Comrade Khaled, would you be ready to go to prison?"

"Yes," I replied without hesitation.

"Will you break down under torture?"

"No."

"Are you ready to die?"

"Yes. Why do you ask these questions? Don't you believe the oath of honour I took?"

"Yes," he muttered apologetically.

"Then let us proceed to the next point," I said impatiently.

He paused as if to make his words more solemn. "Leila, you have a mission to undertake. Go home and say goodbye to your family. Come back tomorrow at ten." I was overjoyed by the news and didn't even dare ask exactly what the mission would be.

At home, mother was most suspicious when I announced that I was going back to Kuwait. She noticed that I had purchased no new clothes and I appeared absorbed in something. Mother said, "Leila, I am going to cook you a real Palestinian dish of Maklouba with Lebanese Kubeh. I have a feeling I am not going to see you for a while, and it's way too early in the summer for you to be going to Kuwait."

I was delighted. "Wonderful, mother, do it. I have truly missed your cooking in the past year." We had a pleasant family meal, but my mind was on the mysterious mission.

In the morning, I left for Beirut. Abu Zeid was waiting. With a glint in his eyes, he calmly said, "Leila, you are going to hijack a TWA plane." I burst out laughing. He was taken aback. "Why are you laughing?" he asked.

"Comrade Abu Zeid," I said, "do you know what passed through my mind when you said that? I imagined I was going to carry the plane on my shoulders and run away with it. I envisioned the guards and all sorts of people running after me."

He replied gravely, "Just get the plane and don't let anyone foil your plan." I rehearsed the whole plan until I had memorised every detail. I was on my way to Rome, not on a romantic adventure, but on a mission against US imperialism.

# 5 Palestine in America

We must grow tough, but without ever losing our tenderness.

*Che Guevara, 1967*

THE ARAB PEOPLE ARE FREQUENTLY ACCUSED by their opponents and sometimes by their friends of being too emotional. I, as a Palestinian Arab woman, have something to be legitimately emotional about: the loss of my home and community and the denial of my present and future. But I am not going to succumb to emotionalism and allow my feelings to blind my reason and undermine my confidence in the capacity of my people to liberate their land.

In spite of the power of the enemy, I intend to rely on revolutionary ideology and strategy and mass mobilization to achieve our objectives. In my work, I have chosen to be the ally of reason, not passion, and my party, the Popular Front, also analyzes and reasons before acting.

We do not embark haphazardly on adventurous and romantic individualistic projects to fulfill "individual needs" or "act out of frustrations and hostilities," as Western "scientific" psychologists hypothesize. We act collectively in a planned manner either to neutralize a prospective friend of the enemy or to expose a vital nerve of the enemy and, above all, to dramatize our own plight and to express our resolute determination to alter "the new realities" that Mr. Moshe Dayan's armies have created.

Generally, we act not with a view to crippling the enemy because we lack the power to do so—but with a view to disseminating revolutionary propaganda, sowing terror in the heart of the enemy, mobilizing our masses, making our cause international, rallying the forces of progress on our side, and underscoring our grievances before an unresponsive Zionist-inspired and Zionist-informed Western public opinion. As a comrade has said: We act heroically in a cowardly world to prove that the enemy is not invincible.

We act "violently" in order to blow the wax out of the ears of the deaf Western liberals and to remove the straws that block their vision. We act as revolutionaries to inspire the masses and to trigger off the revolutionary upheaval in an era of counter-revolution.

Dr. Habash, the Secretary General of the PFLP, has stated our human dilemma and our ethical view thus:

After 22 years of injustice and inhuman living in camps with nobody caring for us, we feel that we have the very full right to protect our revolution; we have all the right to protect our revolution.

Our Code of Morals is Our Revolution. What serves our revolution, what helps our revolution, what protects our revolution is right, is very right and honorable and very noble and very beautiful, because our revolution means justice, means having our homes back, having back our country, which is a very just and noble aim.

(June 12, 1970)

I do not see how my oppressor could sit in judgment on my response to his oppressive actions against me. He is in no position to render an impartial judgment or to accuse me of air piracy and hijacking when he has hijacked my home and hijacked me and my people out of our land. If the enemy defines morality and legality in his own terms and decides to apply his ethical and legal doctrines against me because he has the power as well as the means of communication to justify his inhumanity, I am under no moral obligation to listen, let alone obey his dictates.

Indeed, I am under a moral obligation to resist and to fight to the death the enemy's moral corruption. My deed cannot be evaluated without examining the underlying causes. The revolutionary deed I carried out on August 29, 1969, was an assertion of my spurned humanity, a declaration of the humanity of Palestinians. It was an act of protest against the West for its pro-Zionist (therefore anti-Palestinian) posture. The list of the sins of the West is overwhelming.

Germany, according to Zionism, has "atoned" for the incineration of six million Jews by the payment of nine billion marks in "reparations" to the state of Israel, the "haven" of a united Zionist Jewry. It has since 1965 almost wholly identified with Israel, especially before and during the June War, when the former Nazi chancellor offered to give the Israelis "gas masks" to protect them from "Arab bacteriological warfare." Israel, for her part, has entertained Joseph Strauss and sold Uzzi rifles to Germany.

France has not only supplied Israel with Mystères, Super Mystères, and Mirages, but has allowed the Israelis to "steal" French gunboats from Cherbourg, contrary to De Gaulle's wishes. De Gaulle merely "relieved" the general who turned over the boats to Israel. Guy Mollet, the French Socialist prime minister, conspired with Ben Gurion and Anthony Eden invaded Egypt in 1956. France provided Israel with the scientific know-how and material to manufacture the atomic bomb at Dimona and labeled the plutonium-producing plant a "textile factory."

Switzerland, the neutral country, has not only detained Arab revolutionaries and released the murderers of Palestinians but has also closed its eyes to Zionist kidnappers who killed scientists working for my people. Switzerland has let go practically unpunished Zionists who stole its own state secrets and advanced Mystere blueprints.

England has been guilty of every imaginable crime against my people. Its historic crime is the assassination of my personality, the rape of my land, the obliteration of my history.

America has perpetuated Britain's crimes. It has supplied Israel with Hawk missiles, Skyhawk, and Phantom fighter bombers. America is the defender, apologist, and financier of Israel in every world forum, at every bankers' conference. America is Israel; Israel is America and Europe combined in Palestine.

I do not wish further to burden my reader with our indictment of the West for the crimes it has committed against me and my people, because that alone requires a volume in itself. I merely wish to make some references to the policies of the chief imperialist, America, in order to explain the timing of my revolutionary deed and to illustrate further the bitterness and animosity we harbor towards US imperialism.

On August 29, 1969, Richard Milhous Nixon, the President of the United States, was scheduled to address the 72nd annual meeting of the Zionist Organisation of America. The Popular Front knew what Nixon was going to say because he had said it all before and said it very vociferously when he visited "victorious" Israel in August of 1967 in the aftermath of the June War. He told the Israelis that they would be "foolish to give up any of the territory occupied in the June War without receiving the guarantees of a just peace" that the Israeli leaders were demanding.

Furthermore, Nixon made a joint appearance with Hubert Humphrey before the Jewish B'nai B'rith on September 8, 1968, in Washington. Mr. Humphrey seized this opportunity to make his first formal speech of the election campaign, demonstrating his political loyalty and friendship to "besieged Zion."

Here is an excerpt from Mr. Nixon's speech before B'nai B'rith, the "humanitarian-inclined" Zionist organization:

- **Israel must possess sufficient military power to deter an attack.** As long as the threat of an Arab attack remains direct and imminent, "sufficient power" means the balance must be tipped in Israel's favor. For that reason—to provide Israel a valid self-defense—I support a policy that would give Israel a technological military margin to more than offset her neighbors' numerical superiority.

- **If maintaining that margin should require that the United States supply Israel with Phantom F4 jets, we should supply those jets.** Nixon also stated that "the danger of war increases in direct proportion to the confidence of certain Arab leaders that they could win the war." What generates that confidence and impels the Arabs to think of war is, of course, the Soviet Union, a state that has "stepped up their anti-Semitic propaganda, concocting a 'Zionist plot' in Prague to win support in the Middle East."
- **It is my view that for Israel to take formal and final possession of the occupied territories would be a grave mistake**, but it is not realistic to expect Israel to surrender vital bargaining counters in the absence of a genuine peace and effective guarantees. Israel's enemies can afford to fight and lose and come back to fight again; Israel cannot afford to lose once. America knows that, and America is determined that Israel is here in the family of nations to stay.
- **America supports Israel because we believe in the self-determination of nations.** America supports Israel because we oppose aggression in every form. America supports Israel because its example offers a long-range hope to the Middle East.

Vice President Humphrey, along with Senators Robert F. Kennedy and Eugene McCarthy, had promised to continue military aid to Israel, including jets, until peace was established in the Middle East. Nixon, however, was much more emphatic.

In Houston, Texas, on September 6, 1968, he had declared:

I have the general principle that to maintain the uneasy peace in the Middle East, it is vital that Israel maintain a superiority against its neighbors, and if it takes Phantom jets, then they shall have Phantom jets.

Although we had expected Mr. Nixon to appear in person at the Zionist meeting in Los Angeles on August 29, 1969, as TWA flight 840 took off from Rome, he did not. Instead, he sent a letter to the president, Mr. Jacques Torczyner, who read it to his fellow Zionists on behalf of Mr. Nixon. The letter stated that America was committed to "friendly relations with Israel" and cited the organization "for strengthening Israel's social and economic foundations and the cultural ties between its people and their friends in America." Nixon regarded "these efforts" as being "in the highest American tradition" and assured the Zionists that his government sought "a Middle East arms balance" that favored Israel's "continued military superiority."

As the Zionists were gathering in Los Angeles with California Governor Ronald Reagan and Golda Meir, I was having a pleasant chat with the Singer Sewing Machine Company's Middle East agent on my way to Rome to divert TWA flight 840 to Damascus.

I had trained for every conceivable contingency; I had mastered most operational details of the great Boeing 707. There was something, however, I did not train for: the human situation. How to deal with idle or curious conversationalists. How not to arouse their suspicions or be rude to a seatmate.

I had to improvise and felt very uncomfortable. I imagined that all the Westerners aboard knew about my mission.

My seatmate from Beirut to Rome was a clean-cut, sociable American on his way to New York. I knew that Americans, like most other tourists, like to make casual conversation about everything under the sun. I didn't realize that they posed personal questions so directly and so nonchalantly. Mr. Holden must have been bored, and he wanted to talk.

"Where are you going?" he asked to open the conversation.

"I am going to Rome," I said.

"Why are you going to Rome?" he continued.

I paused momentarily to fabricate an answer and said with simulated shyness, "I am going to meet my fiancé, who is coming from London to meet me in Rome in a few days." I suddenly realized I had made a slip. What if he too were going to Rome and asked me to dinner or something while I was waiting for my "fiancé"? I swiftly corrected my mistake by adding, "It is quite possible that he might surprise me and be waiting for me at the airport."

Then I asked him, "Where are you going?"

"To New York," he said, much to my relief. He was determined not to let the conversation lapse.

"How on earth would an Arab girl be going to Rome to meet her fiancé alone and get married?" he asked.

I answered in a superficially self-assured tone, "I've known him since we were children, and we've been engaged for several years; besides, we are modern, not traditional Arabs."

"That's good," he said and started telling me how he and his wife had eloped because her parents had disapproved of him.

As I assured him that I was not eloping, the stewardess cheerfully announced that there was a newly married couple on the plane and they had a huge cake they would like us to share. "Who would like to have some cake?" she said.

Everybody, including Mr. Holden and I, chanted in a chorus of "I would." In the midst of this jolly atmosphere, Mr. Holden asked, as if to dampen my enthusiasm for marriage, "How come you're getting married when your fiancé is still a student and without a career?"

I smiled. "We're not filthy rich oil kings, but we're rich enough to afford it while we're young."

"Then," he said, "may I suggest that you spend your honeymoon on a yacht by yourselves on a Mediterranean cruise?"

I interrupted, protesting, "I'd rather be among people."

He slyly asked, "Are you going to marry the people?"

"No," I said, "but I love being with people."

As I cleared customs and claimed my luggage, I had to face a porter who insisted on helping me and then asked, "When can I see you - tonight?" I was angered by his forwardness and firmly said, "I am engaged; I am sorry," resorting to the traditional stewardess's reply. I had to face the same problem with another man on the bus into Rome. By now, I was running out of patience, especially as my suitor squeezed close to me and practically tried to hold me in his arms without having spoken to me.

I said furiously, "Take your hand off me. You're about to drive me out of the bus with your pushiness." He did, and he didn't dare make any other overtures all the way.

I spent two days at the hotel fending off invitations for personally guided tours of Rome. During these two days, I walked the streets of Rome alone. It is strange, but I had no desire to purchase anything, see Rome's ancient glory, or even go to a film. I only walked and walked, contemplating my mission and reciting its details to myself.

Early on the morning of August 29, I checked out of the hotel and caught a bus to Fiumicino Airport on the outskirts of Rome. Happily, the only snag was a half-hour flight delay. My associate, whom I recognized only from a photograph, appeared on schedule and we exchanged pre-arranged signals.

His name was Salim Issawi; he was a Palestinian from Haifa who had been raised in Syria. Salim sat quietly nearby, and we tried to ignore each other. All was going smoothly when suddenly the human element threatened our careful planning. A few seats away, there was a little girl with a button on her dress cheerfully proclaiming, "Make Friends."

That message brought me up short, forced me to remind myself, as I watched her playing with her little sister, that this child had committed no crime against me or my people. It would be cruel to imperil her life by hijacking a plane, the symbolic meaning of which she had no conception—a plane that could explode during our attempted seizure or be blown up by Israeli anti-aircraft fire when we entered the "Israeli airspace."

While these qualms pricked my conscience, the whole history of Palestine and her children came before my eyes. I saw everything from the first day of my exile. I saw my people homeless, hungry, barefoot. The twice "refugee" children of Bagan camp near Amman seemed to stand, a humiliated multitude, in front of me saying, "We too are children, and we are a part of the human race."

The scene strengthened me enormously. I said to myself, "What crime did I and my people perpetrate against anyone to deserve the fate we have suffered?" The answer was "None." The operation must be carried out. There can be no doubt or retreat. My children have spoken.

On the bus across the field to the Boeing 707, another unscheduled problem developed. A handsome man in his early thirties came up to me and said, "Hello" in a most jovial, enthusiastic manner.

"Hello," I replied nonchalantly, as I calmly tried to read *My Friend Che* by Ricardo Rojo. He seemed very eager to talk and asked me who I was and where I was going. I couldn't very well repeat the marriage tale and couldn't invent anything quickly enough. I said, "Guess."

He tried, "Greek, Spanish, Italian?" I asked him where he was from.

"I am from Chicago," he answered, and continued his questioning. "You wouldn't be South American, would you?" Now that I knew where he was from, I figured it was safe to say that I was a South American. I thought it might end his questioning, at least.

"From Brazil?" he asked, looking admiringly at me and ogling my whole body.

"You're getting closer," I said.

"Bolivia?"

"Yes," I replied, "but how did you know?"

"It's your book that gave you away," he declared. I asked him what he thought of Che.

"Good man," he said.

"Where are you going?" I countered, trying to change to a less controversial topic.

"To Athens, to see my mother. I haven't seen her in fifteen years. I bet she's there already, waiting for me at the airport."

I was astounded and almost told him, "You bloody fool, you'd better get off this plane because it isn't going to Athens." I tried to ignore him and closed my ears to keep his voice from penetrating my inner conscience. I plunged into a nervous reading of *My Friend Che*.

This encounter made me stop and think because I understood the longing for one's own country. However, I rationalized his plight by making a distinction between his "exile," which was voluntary, and mine, which was forced. But these human encounters made me decide to be extra careful not to jeopardize the lives of the passengers unnecessarily. Their welfare, however, did not and could not cripple my operation. The deed had to be carried out. There was no turning back.

The plane was airborne for only twenty minutes before the hostesses were graciously trying to serve their five first-class passengers. Neither Salim nor I was anxious to eat. The stewardesses were very solicitous. They offered us drinks and peanuts—anything we wanted. I settled for a coffee, Salim for a beer. But they made us nervous, as they kept returning and asking us if we wanted anything else. I pretended that I had a stomach ache and asked for a blanket.

I innocently placed it over my lap so I could take my hand grenade out of my purse and put my pistol right in the top of my trousers without being noticed. Salim asked for an aspirin tablet. I was afraid the stewardess might suspect something had she realized that two passengers opposite each other in the first row were sick. In any case, I dreaded the prospect of having a companion with a headache, so I was relieved when he merely pocketed the aspirin.

Seconds after the only other male passenger in the first-class section returned from the small lounge, I gestured to Salim to proceed to the cockpit. Just at that moment, another hostess carrying the crew's lunch trays was opening the door of the cockpit.

Salim seized the opportunity and leapt in ahead of her. She screamed, "Oh no!" and her trays flew in the air, causing much noise but no injury. I was behind Salim and ordered the stewardess to get out of the way. She did, quivering and watching us over her shoulder.

Salim was so huge that he blocked my view, and I couldn't see the reaction of the crew. I could, however, hear him say that the plane had been taken over by the Che Guevara Commando Unit of the PFLP and announce that the new captain was Shadiah Abu Ghazalah.

In the middle of his speech, my pistol slipped down the leg of my trousers. As I bent down to pick it up, I saw the bewildered looks on the crew's faces. I suppose all they could see was part of my wide-brimmed chic hat. I felt ridiculous for a moment, laughed at my ineptness, put the pistol away, and entered the cockpit solemnly brandishing my hand grenade and declaring I was the new captain.

The crew was completely shocked to see me there, but they showed no fear. To demonstrate my credibility, I immediately offered my predecessor, Captain Carter, the safety pin from the grenade as a souvenir. He respectfully declined it. I dropped it at his feet and made my speech: "If you obey my orders, all will be well; if not, you will be responsible for the safety of passengers and aircraft."

"Go to Lydda," I instructed.

"To Lod?" he queried, using the Israeli name.

"You understand English, don't you?" I said curtly. "You just listen to my orders and don't ask silly questions."

Since I knew the plane carried fuel for almost three hours and 45 minutes, I decided to reaffirm my authority by testing the flight engineer. I turned towards him and asked, "How much fuel do you have, flight engineer?"

"For two hours," he promptly replied, without even looking at the fuel gauge.

"Liar," I shouted, and told him that I knew just as much as he did about the Boeing, and that if he ever lied to me again, I'd break his neck. The pilot tried to calm me down. He thought I was angry, but I was actually overjoyed. He warned the crew not to be obstinate in dealing with their new captain.

Realizing that he was prepared to cooperate, I asked Captain Carter to radio Rome so that I could explain my actions to the Italian people. He explained that we were too far away. I insisted that he try. He did, but we had no luck.

I asked a steward to bring our hand luggage forward and then ordered him and the other first-class passengers to move to the tourist section. Next, I demanded that the intercom system be turned on. All orders were complied with, and I read the following message to the passengers:

---

Ladies and gentlemen, your attention please. Kindly fasten your seat belts. This is your new captain speaking. The Che Guevara Commando Unit of the Popular Front for the Liberation of Palestine, which has taken over command of this TWA flight, demands that all passengers on board adhere to the following instructions:

1. Remain seated and keep calm.
2. For your own safety, place your hands behind your head.
3. Make no move which would endanger the lives of other passengers on this plane.

We will consider all your demands within the safe limits of our plan. Among you is a passenger responsible for the death and misery of a number of Palestinian men, women, and children, on behalf of whom we are carrying out this operation to bring this assassin before a revolutionary Palestinian court. The rest of you will be honorable guests of the heroic Palestinian people in a hospitable, friendly country. Every one of you, regardless of religion or nationality, is guaranteed freedom to go wherever he pleases as soon as the plane is safely landed. Our destination is a friendly country, and friendly people will receive you.

---

As I completed reading the message, I observed that the plane had swerved off the course I charted for it. I ordered the captain not to play games if he wanted to reach our destination safely and put him on course again.

Then Salim reminded me that fifteen minutes had elapsed since the passengers were asked to hold their hands behind their heads. I quickly advised them to relax and to drink champagne if they so desired and offered an apology for inconveniencing them.

Shortly afterward, a stewardess came in and explained that most of the passengers didn't understand English, didn't know what we had said, and would like us to repeat the message.

She even offered to translate it into French for them. I repeated the message and assured them that everything was normal, that there was only one person on the plane we were after.

Later, this was interpreted by the press as indicating that we were after the Israeli ambassador to the US, General Itzhak Rabin of June War fame. We were not, and if we had been, I would not have boarded flight 840 at Rome, since I saw all the passengers and knew that Rabin was not among them. Saleh Al Moualim, an Israeli Arab on board, must have thought that he was the person we meant because he became very jittery and frightened.

The selective terror tactic worked; the passengers' fear diminished and everyone cooperated with us. In explaining the message to the passengers, I told them that we detested the American government's Middle East actions and held no grudge against any individual person. They were frightened, however, when I announced that we intended to blow up the plane upon arrival in a friendly country. I announced this only an hour before reaching Damascus.

Meanwhile, I resumed radio contact with the ground, sending messages of solidarity to the Greek revolutionaries and to the people of South Europe. I demanded that the Greek colonels release our imprisoned revolutionaries and said that the CIA plotters would be toppled by the Greek people.

All went according to plan until we got the Egyptian observation tower on our wavelength. I identified myself to the controller in Arabic and asked him to convey to the Egyptian people the greetings of the Palestinian revolution.

I advised him that I was going to Lydda, and his voice crackled: "Allah, to Lydda, what will you do there?"

"Visit the fatherland," I said.

"Are you sure of that?"

"I certainly am," I replied enthusiastically.

He tried to tell me that it was too dangerous. I switched him off, then relented momentarily as he screamed, "Oh Front, Oh Popular, Oh Arab Palestine!" but the rest of the appeal was too incoherent and inaudible.

Within minutes, I could see the coast of my Palestine in the haze. As we approached the land of my birth, it seemed that my love and I were racing towards each other for an eternal embrace. I rushed towards my beloved and saw Palestine for the first time since my forced exile in 1948. I was lost in a moment of passion and meditation.

Then I remembered the mission and ordered the pilot to descend. I addressed a message in Arabic to my fellow exiles in occupied Palestine, telling them we shall return and we shall recover the land. I advised them to remain steadfast and promised to smash the Zionist fortress of conceit.

I told Lydda tower in Arabic that we were going to land. The pilot said he didn't understand and told us we should ask for clearance and wait. I said, "This is my country. I do not need permission from the Zionist vultures to land."

I spoke to the tower in English, saying, "Here we come again. Shadiah Abu Ghaselah has come back to life. There are millions of Shadiahs who will be returning again and again to reclaim the land." The Israeli tower must have been terrified for a while because I said that we intended to blow up the plane right in the airport. In seconds, three Israeli Mirages appeared on the horizon and tried to prevent us from landing. I turned the intercom on so that the passengers could hear the exchange.

I declared anew that the pilot and the Israelis were responsible for the safety of the passengers and the plane, and that we intended to do no harm to anyone if our orders were obeyed. The co-pilot asked if he could speak to the Israelis, and I let him.

He said, "Popular Front, Free Arab Palestine, armed people have threatened to explode the plane with hand grenades if your Mirages don't clear out." Until this moment, the Israeli tower was still addressing us as TWA 840. My patience ran out, and I told him to shut up and turned him off, saying that there would be no further communications until he addressed us as Popular Front, Free Arab Palestine.

In seconds, he did so as we swung around my beloved Haifa. The pilot asked, "What shall I do now?" I said, "Let's take a seven-minute tour of the fatherland." My father's image appeared before my eyes, and I could hear his voice saying.

"When will we return home?" My whole world came together. I was silent. I looked out at the greenery and mountains of Palestine. I could see Tel Aviv below.

I wept out of affection and longing and said softly, "Father, we shall return. We shall redeem your honour and restore your dignity. We shall become the sovereign of the land someday."

Suddenly, I remembered that the mission preceded personal emotions. I instructed the pilot, "Go to Lebanon, where my people live as refugees." The Israeli planes continued to pursue us. At the Lebanese border, they zoomed away. I called Cyprus and sent greetings to its heroic anti-imperialist fighters and sent messages to my people in South Lebanon. The pilot interrupted.

"We must ask for clearance from Beirut."

"We don't need to ask for clearance," I said. "This is an Arab country." We circled Beirut briefly before I ordered the pilot to go on to Damascus.

He objected, "The airport there couldn't accommodate the Boeing 707."

"Look, do you think we're so backward that we couldn't handle your damned plane?" I said strongly. He didn't respond. I took the microphone and addressed the passengers for the last time: "Evacuate immediately on landing; have a happy holiday in Syria. I trust we shall have a smooth landing."

The fuel gauge was reading empty; the pilot sought clearance, and I ordered him to land immediately on the runway farthest from the air terminal. "Let's have a smooth landing," I said, "because if I fall, the hand grenade could explode, and that would be a terrible anticlimax to a happy journey."

He landed smoothly, and in less than three minutes, the plane was empty. Salim and I tried to tell the passengers to slow down and to take their personal belongings with them. Most ran out barefooted. Even the crew left their jackets behind.

As Captain Carter stepped out, I saluted and thanked him for his cooperation. He looked at me in astonishment.

The co-pilot said, "You're most welcome."

I checked the plane. All the passengers had left. Salim wired the cockpit and lit the fuse. I slid out on one of the torn emergency chutes and fell to the ground on my rear. Salim followed and landed on my shoulders.

The plane did not explode as scheduled. Salim's personal courage made him climb back in and set everything in motion once more. When Syrian soldiers arrived on the scene, I distracted them by saying, "The Israeli officers ran in that direction. Go and get them." Salim was still in the plane. I feared for his safety but admired his heroism and selfless devotion. I tried to leap in and couldn't. Suddenly, he appeared and waved reassuringly. The Boeing still did not explode.

He fired a few shots into the wing of the plane, but there was no fuel left, so it wouldn't readily ignite. When sparks finally fluttered, we took cover twenty yards away. Half a mile away, the passengers in the terminal watched the bonfire and the explosion of the Boeing. The Syrian soldiers returned, astounded. They were even more surprised when Salim and I surrendered to them and turned over our weapons. The Al-Hadaf photographer, who was parachuted by the Front to film our landing and the explosion, was so excited that he forgot to remove the lens cap from his camera.

Our Syrian hosts took us to the air terminal, where I delivered a brief speech to the passengers:

Ladies and gentlemen, thank you for your kind attention and cooperation during the flight. I am Captain Shadiah Abu Ghazalah. That's not my name; my name is Khaleda. Shadiah is an immortal woman who wrote: "Heroes are often forgotten, but their legends and memories are the property and heritage of the people."

That is something historians and analysts cannot understand. Shadiah will not be forgotten by the Popular Front and by the generation of revolutionaries she helped mold in the path of revolution. I would like you to know that Shadiah was a Palestinian Arab woman from Nablus; that she was a schoolteacher and a member of the Popular Front underground; that she died in an explosion at her own home at the age of twenty-one on November 21, 1968, while manufacturing hand grenades for the Front. She was the first woman martyr of our revolution.

I assumed her name on flight 840 to tell the world about the crimes the Israelis inflict upon our people and to demonstrate to you that they make no distinctions between men, women, and children. But for their own propaganda objectives, they repeatedly state in your press how we attack their "innocent" women and children and how cruel we are.

I want you to know that we love children, too, and we certainly do not aim our guns at them. We diverted flight 840 because TWA is one of the largest American airlines that services the Israeli air routes and, more importantly, because it is an American plane. The American government is Israel's staunchest supporter. It supplies Israel with weapons for our destruction. It gives the Zionists tax-free American dollars. It supports Israel at world conferences. It helps them in every possible way.

We are against America because she is an imperialist country. Our unit is called the Che Guevara Commando Unit because we abhor America's assassination of Che and because we are a part of the Third World and the world revolution. Che was an apostle of that revolution.

We took the plane to Haifa because Comrade Salim and I come from Haifa. Both of us were evicted in 1948. We took you to Tel Aviv as an act of defiance and challenge to the Israelis and to demonstrate their impotence when the Arabs embark on an offensive rather than defensive strategy. We brought you to Damascus because Syria is the pulsating heart of the Arab homeland and because the Syrians are a good and generous people.

We hope you will enjoy your stay in Damascus. We hope you will go home and tell your friends not to go to Israel—to the Middle East war zone. Please tell your neighbors that we are a people like you who wish to live in peace and security in our country, governing ourselves.

Please tell the Americans that if they hate war and the exploitation of others, they should stop their government from making war on us and helping the Israelis to deprive us of our land. Tell your people that coming to Israel helps her to deny our rights.

Revolution and peace. Greetings to all lovers of the oppressed!

It was nearly seven p.m., August 29, 1969. As I concluded my speech, I saw my Greek friend sobbing and an American woman trying to assuage him. I do not think he recognized me as his bus companion. Salim and I mixed with the passengers and distributed sweets to the children. Two old ladies were consoling each other; one was saying she was "wet," and the other was telling her to thank God for having arrived in Damascus alive.

The Syrian authorities cleared the passengers through customs and took them to hotels in Damascus. They released all of them with the exception of six Israelis.

One American woman was taken to the hospital with a broken ankle. On September 3, four Israelis were released; later, the other two were exchanged for two Syrian air force pilots in Israeli custody and a handful of imprisoned fighters. Salim and I were taken to police headquarters.

Although we had arrived at the airport to the cheers of the Syrian crowds, the Syrian officials were not that friendly. An arrogant colonel started his investigation by demanding, "What do you think you are?"

"Soldiers, like you," I said.

"No," he angrily replied, "you are a terrorist organization."

"Hey," I said, "am I in Israel or the Syrian Arab Republic, the advocate of revolutionary warfare?"

The colonel didn't like my tone of voice. "This action is not fedayeen-like. It is terrorism," he said.

"Look," I explained, "I am a soldier who carried out her assignment. If you wish to debate the validity and legitimacy of our revolutionary strategy, we'll be happy to do it with you, but not in a police station."

"Where did you train?"

"I will answer no further questions, since I already gave you my name and told you what party I belong to."

The colonel ordered us to be held in dingy little rooms and gave us two blankets each. At about eleven-thirty p.m., we were taken from our cells to the second floor for further interrogation. I gave my name as Khaleda, and they obviously knew it was false. The officer in charge was rather suave and clever. He ordered his assistants to bring us dinner and proceeded to tell us how he strongly identified with the Palestine revolution.

I interrupted, "That is not the colonel's view."

"What colonel?" he said.

"You should know," I answered.

The assistants brought food, and I declined it.

Declaring, "I won't eat until I am released."

"Where will you go if released?" he asked.

"To my country, Palestine," I said. The officer inquired about many things, and my answer was an emphatic "No comment" to every question.

Late that night, I asked to go to the bathroom, and I was accompanied by a male policeman who was under orders to search me before I went in. I dared him to touch me and threatened to attack him and scream rape if he did. He ignored the orders and took me back to my windowless cell. I asked the male guard to buy me a packet of cigarettes; he refused, doling out one cigarette at a time for the remainder of the night. Since I was unable to sleep, see anyone, or talk, I kept the guard marching me back and forth to the bathroom all night. I do not know who was more exhausted by morning. I continued that strategy for the next four nights.

On the morning of August 31, breakfast was brought in, and I declined to eat again, announcing that I was on a hunger strike. By then, I hadn't had a good meal in three days, and I was smoking very heavily. I was also getting bored being in isolation but knowing full well that my comrades were joyously celebrating my deed. Around noon, I twisted the edge of the rusty iron partition between me and Salim, and we started whispering to each other face to face.

I told him about the "wet lady" at the airport, and we laughed boisterously about it. The guard heard the noise and ran towards the cell, thinking I must have gone mad. He asked me to share the joke with him. I refused to say anything. But when he realized that I was still sane, he looked around my cell and found the hole.

He accused me of being a terrorist and threatened dire consequences if I widened the hole. I dared him, "Go and tell your superiors."

That afternoon, another colonel came to visit us, but he was in civilian clothes. He was smoother than his predecessors. He introduced himself as a Palestinian pilot with the Syrian air force from Al-Nassera.

"My name is Azzani," he said, "and I have just returned from the front bringing you the revolutionary greetings of the fighters."

I said, "If you recognize us as revolutionaries, why are you holding us in prison?"

"Why are you on a hunger strike?" he asked, without answering my question.

I said, "Because I am being treated like a criminal, and I protest very strongly against these insulting interrogations of intelligence officers like yourself." He asked if I needed anything or any money. I replied proudly, "I have money, and the only thing I want is departure from this Baath prison."

He left without comment.

On September 1, I felt very weak and tired.

Stomach ache, headache, and general fatigue seemed to have overtaken me. I began to feel dizzy, but I still refused to eat. That evening, I fainted on my way to the bathroom, and it took them a few minutes to revive me. The Syrians were very disturbed and called in a doctor who tried to persuade me to eat some yogurt or drink something other than coffee. I insisted "No" and passed out again. All I remember after that was a nurse bathing my face and Salim carrying me to a hospital ambulance. I was not fully conscious until the morning of September 2, when, with a sense of inner peace and self-fulfillment, I sat down in the hospital and wrote a few notes, taking my inspiration from Che's immortal dictum: "We must grow tough, but

without ever losing our tenderness."

"What a beautiful passage, but more beautiful is the tradition of revolutionary tenderness. I am not sure that I have practiced that art effectively. Others will have to pass judgment on my deed. I am certain, though, that the capitalist press regarded my deed as an 'outrage' and urged their governments to prosecute those criminals ruthlessly or to extradite them to other countries where they could be prosecuted.

"I am somewhere in Damascus. I was placed here after I carried out my mission. After I performed my revolutionary duty against the enemy." It was a momentous second in my life when I put my fingers on the trigger and ordered the enemy to obey my command. All my life, I dreamt of carrying arms to aim at the enemy—that vengeful enemy who raped our land and has expropriated our homes without compensation.

"Oh Palestine! I am ready to die, and I shall live by dying for thee!

"Oh my homeland! My love, my only love! I shall revolt against thine enemies, all enemies. I shall make bombs from the atoms of my body and weave a new Palestine from the fabric of my soul.

With all my power and the power of my sisters, we shall convert our existence into bombs to redeem the land, the coast, the mountain. We shall fight and fight.

"Oh! I seem to be forgetting myself. I am writing as if I were a poet. Poetry is also part of our armory, but deeds are a sharper aspect of our weaponry.

"Oh God! When will the deprivation end? When will I return to my home—to embrace life in its fullest? There in Haifa, I shall live, for I feel choked here.

"I feel oversatiated for having beaten the CIA. And why not? Hadn't Salim Issawi and I hit at the heart of America and its power? Let America give Israel all the weapons she requests. I am sure my people shall live. I am in the observation tower, and nothing frightens me. My people are being steeled by struggle against the imperialist and Zionist enemies.

"I remember the moment I entered the pilot's cabin and how he shivered before me. How the words of surrender flowed from his lips: 'O.K., all right. I'll do whatever you want. Now tell me what to do.'

"He was stunned by my deed. I am certain he cursed Israel and America a thousand times in the silence of his heart. "What an exciting occasion to force every air tower, including that of Israel, to broadcast our slogans: `Popular Front, Free Arab Palestine.'

"The pilot was the first to shout our slogan. He said it with a quivering voice. He is a middle-class American who was taught to love himself more than anything else. I have no doubts that selfishness is an American virtue that manifests itself when Americans are not acting collectively under a victorious leadership. I remember how they fled from the Japanese and how they retreated like sheep in the Far East. I don't think the pilot cared to sacrifice himself for America.

"What a splendid moment in my life when I flew over the homeland in an enemy plane. Oh, my God! What a beautiful land. I felt like landing and dying at the hands of my enemy. To land, to melt into the eternity of the land, and to form part of the soil of Palestine but our revolutionary nobility impelled me to sacrifice my personal wishes for a union with the land in order to save the children who committed no sin against me or my people. The passengers are not guilty of any crime. As for our part, aren't we the friends of all peoples?

Now I remember the moment I communicated with Cairo and conveyed our revolutionary greetings to the Egyptian Arab people. The Cairo tower wanted to know where we were heading. I told him Lydda.

`Lord, no!' he said.

`Yes, Lydda,' I said. 'God! - and what are you going to do there?

'We are going for a visit,' I said.

"Moments after, I was in touch with the Lydda tower, which insisted on calling me TWA 840. I told him sternly to shut up and refused to answer him until he addressed me: Popular Front, Free Arab Palestine - exacting such concessions from a Zionist stooge was indeed an achievement. "The Israelis thought that Salim and I were going to explode the plane and its passengers. What fools! They must think we're a bunch of suicidal gangsters like their leaders.

"In Damascus, we indeed exploded the cockpit of the imperialist plane as an expression of our strategy, which aims at hitting the imperialist interests wherever they may be. The Popular Front will destroy the treasonous enemy - the enemy of humanity, right, and justice. Blessed be the arms that carry out deeds and the revolutionary brains that conceive of deeds and plan them. We shall be victorious.

"Sleep has fled from my eyes. I hear the cries of prisoners being tortured in Syrian dungeons. I cannot condone torture, no matter what the crime was. I hate to hear of a man crying in pain. I hate the infliction of pain on any person because I know what it is to feel pain—pain and anguish for the loss of the homeland, for the loss of a whole people, the pain of my entire nation. Pain truly affects my soul; so does the persecution of my people. It is from pain that I derive the power to resist and to defend the persecuted.

"My people, my land, my Palestine! For thee I shall resist; for your honor, I shall accept pain. Palestine, my love! For you, I shall fight, fight and open the road—the road of return, victorious return to all parents, to all lovers.

Today I am a volcano, a revolutionary volcano, the Front-Volcano, the Front-revolution. Yes—the revolt of return.

My Front is free. My Front to Palestine, paving the way to all, to all my Arab people with guns, cannons—my Front acts and with brains.

Yes, with brains we act, act, act! I reflected briefly and wrote a note to my mother, to my mother and to all mothers."

"To you, my dearest, I write these lines. Where are you? I see you only in my imagination ... you are waiting for my return ... be patient, Mother ... I shall return ... I see you, beloved, in the hands of thine enemies ... I am choking ... on the verge of death every time I imagine you ... "Oh Lord, safeguard her and safeguard my people as you protected me. Safeguard them from the persecution of the enemy. Blind the enemy whenever he tries to violate my domicile for my Palestine is not only my mother ... she is my sister, friend, and companion.

"Oh, how I long for Palestine, for my beloved, for my brothers and sisters in this little Syrian cage where I feel physically bound and spiritually boundless and universal, for I have overcome the particular and reached for the true good—the good of the oppressed.

"The feeling of being uprooted accompanies me everywhere; the feeling of being stateless, without a homeland, is a feeling that can only be obliterated by the return! Oh, Lord, what a dreadful human dilemma to be separated forcefully from one's own country!

"Yes, I feel unanchored ... for my land is raped ... it is under the hoofs of the Zionists ... a people that have evicted my mother and other mothers and raped my true Mother Palestine.

"I swear by my revolution, by my humanity, that we shall return the Palestinians to their homes and we shall recover our lost humanity!" Yes, we have lost everything: we have lost life and its meaning; we have lost the humanity of man; we are a people that lost their land; and he who loses his land loses his life—for land is the source of life.

My beloved, I shall return on the wings of eagles to you; I shall return repeatedly to spread terror in the heart of the enemy. I shall flag the enemy; I shall pulverize him.

And why not? How can I forget the rage of the tempest that struck my dear father ... a thousand greetings I send to your soul, my father, and the souls of Palestinian fathers in the beyond. Tortured, you left Palestine and uprooted you lived; desire replaced health, sadness joy, hatred love, humiliation pride.

Father, rest assured I shall avenge your honor and redeem your dignity the honor and dignity of all martyrs!

By cannons, bullets, bayonets! From the heavens we shall descend, from the sea we shall come, from Mount Carmel we shall leap to the heart of Haifa. My Front shall do this to tend the wounded, succor the needy and inspire the children of despair. Mother, I can no longer keep my secret: I am a lover of Palestine, and I have no other love ...

Therefore remain firm and constant unafraid my people face tyranny and oppression. Be with me, my beloved, remember our martyrs, remember the stolen lands.

Take all difficulties with steadfast revolutionary violence!

For the path is long and steep and the recovery of the homeland needs absolute firmness.

Henceforth we shall not bend our heads. The enemy may be strong ... but we are much stronger.

Our cause is right and just and we have begun to believe in ourselves.

We no longer know fear.

Wait for me. Wait for victory.

We shall return!"

On September 3, I was shocked to hear that the Syrians had released four Israelis while Salim and I were still detained. I lashed out at the Syrians, threatening retaliation. The nurses tried to calm me, explaining that the hospital was not a prison and urging me to eat if I wanted to be released quickly.

I promised to behave if they brought me newspapers and let me listen to the radio. They agreed, and I felt compensated for my fatigue when I heard a broadcast in which the story of the hijacking was told according to the pilot. Moments later, the Commander-in-Chief of the Syrian armed forces, General Mustafa Tlass, entered my room—my most distinguished visitor. The General said he disapproved strongly of my deed and insinuated that I was a UAR agent who had brought the plane to Syria to embarrass the Syrians and give President Nasser a propaganda boost.

I assured him that the Front was totally autonomous and took orders from no one. I raised the issue of the released Israelis, and he explained that I was "the guest, not the prisoner of Syria."

"I would rather not be anybody's guest because I must return to my base to carry on with my work," I said, and asked him to see if he could arrange a meeting for me with President Attassi.

The President was in Egypt for a meeting of the front-line states, he explained, and he didn't know when he was coming back.

The General left, and Salim and I were moved to an apartment with four other people. We began to realize that the more indignant we behaved, the more lenient and accommodating the Syrians became. We demanded to know why we were being kept there and how long it was going to continue. There was no reply. Around ten that evening, we were visited by Colonel Ali Zaza (he is presently the Minister of the Interior under President Hafez Al-Assad) and got an inkling of what was in store for us. Zaza came with two other men who identified themselves as Saiga commanders. (Saiga is the Syrian-supported section of the resistance.) They were eager to talk.

For the next four hours, we debated the whole history of the resistance, the role of Fateh, the Palestine National Congress and its value, and the nature of socialism. It became increasingly obvious that Saiga was a branch of the Syrian Baath and had no independent personality of its own. Although we agreed on some points, we felt that, on the whole, the Baath of Attassi, Jedid, and Makkous (the current ruling triumvirate of Syria) believed in left-wing Baathism, not scientific socialism and dialectical materialism.

By September 4, we must have become very fashionable and respectable. Four ladies of upper-class appearance and attitudes came to visit us and presented me with a bouquet of flowers. Three introduced themselves as representatives of the Syrian, Palestinian, and Lebanese Union of Women, and one as a member of Fateh. I looked at them with contempt and asked if their bouquet was a fitting tribute to a living revolutionary who had accomplished her mission. They were taken aback.

One had the audacity to criticize the Front for the operation, calling it an attempt on our part to eclipse the burning of the Al-Aksa mosque, an action that was gaining sympathy for the Arabs and unifying the Moslem world behind one policy. (At one hurriedly called summit conference of Arab states, Israel was held responsible for the burning of the mosque and accused of desecrating a Moslem shrine and attempting to Judaize it.)

I explained that the Al-Aksa incident had occurred more than a week before our attack and had no relation to our action. Furthermore, I insisted, we did not strive for a unity based on religious bigotry, but we were fighting for the unity of the anti-imperialist forces. My congenial guests were not impressed. They were upset that an "upstart" like myself could dare cast aspersions on their idols. They walked out in a huff, never to return to amuse me with their feminine slave passions and fashions.

The evening of September 4 was a sad one for me. I learned of the death of a great revolutionary leader, Ho Chi Minh. Ho's death struck me like lightning. I felt part of me had died. It was the same feeling as when I heard about the assassination of Che. I knew Ho's principles would live and that he was an old man who had lived a full life and helped liberate a substantial part of his homeland.

Yet I was sad and contemplated for an entire sleepless night the greatness of Ho and what we Palestinians could learn from him and his example. The next morning, I sat down and wrote a poem.

During a five-week period, from September 5 until October 11, Salim and I were held in three different "guest houses" in Syria. The Syrians, I am certain, were not afraid of Salim or me. They feared the Front and its heroic exploits. They must have remembered vividly how Dr. Habash, whom they imprisoned in 1968, was "kidnapped" with his Syrian guards by the Front from the most guarded security prison in Syria.

The Syrians moved us around constantly in the hope of averting a similar "kidnapping." However, our "kidnapping" was never contemplated because our continued imprisonment in Syria was considered an effective indictment of a regime that proclaimed itself a revolutionary proponent of people's wars and at the same time thwarted revolutionary operations. The Syrians considered themselves somewhat accommodating as they fulfilled some of their "guests'" desires.

They took us to the airport and allowed us to take some pictures of the Boeing 707. We also visited a number of places in Damascus, including the hated symbol of our defeat, Bloodan Palace, from whence had emanated the call of the Arab leadership to end the general strike of 1936—an action that sealed the fate of Palestine and enabled the British and Zionists to wipe out the revolutionary cadres of that era.

We had to demand, threaten, and fight in order to ameliorate the social conditions under which we lived and the tight security that surrounded us. On three different occasions, we had to go on hunger strikes. We were permitted to see some visitors, but we had no freedom of movement nor opportunity to communicate with associates. I felt lonely and confined. Salim was furious, and it was hard for me to accept emotionally the fact that I was in an "Arab prison," although we had considered the possibility before embarking on our mission. I seemed to have become self-centered; yet I wanted to express my social concern—to reach for a loftier future. I turned to writing.

How miserable can one become when one thinks only of oneself and no others?

How despondent can one become when one imagines that one is the third pivot of the world; how insipid life becomes when one remembers that one's life is coming to an end. Oh my soul, how I hate your rebelliousness when all of me aches.

Be merciful, my soul, for a moment.

Have I not been your obedient slave?

I feel a very strange feeling ... how childish!

I long for love ... love ... love.

I shall resist this longing, but I am overcome; I shall hearken to the voice of love.

I shall embrace my beloved and sleep.

I am in union with my humanity - with Palestine.

On October 11, 1969, Salim and I visited the then Syrian minister of defence (now President), Hafez Al-Assad. We had spent forty-five days under house arrest, cut off from the world. I regarded our stay in Damascus as an internment. Al-Assad adhered to the official policy of giving us "hospitality." When I persisted in calling myself a prisoner of the Syrian Baath, the minister apologetically explained that his government was under external pressure either to extradite us or put us on trial. Both alternatives, he said, were highly unpalatable. He expressed grudging admiration for us while insinuating that the operation was the work of Egyptian intelligence against "revolutionary" Syria, the implication that provoked me to say that the wretched Arab intelligence system was quite incapable of thinking of, let alone executing, such daring operations.

"Besides, Mr. Minister," I asserted, "you should know that's false because Arab intelligence services are well informed on the affairs of other Arab states."

Al-Assad then asked, "Why did you elect to land in Syria?"—implying that our action was in retaliation for the Syrian detention of Dr. Habash, the Secretary General of the Front.

My reply was, "Principally for practical reasons. First, we were short on fuel; and second, what difference did it make whether we landed in Egypt or Syria? Aren't you both progressive Arab states?" The minister was not pleased with my stress on the word "progressive." I reminded him that Colonel Zaza had promised to obtain our release some time ago and to arrange for an interview with President Attassi. Moreover, I declared, I didn't see any reasons why we should be kept in this dungeon while the Israelis were set free.

He was disturbed and said, "You are free to go, Khaleda," using the pseudonym I insisted on using while I was held in Syria. Within minutes, Salim and I were ready to depart. Al Assad offered to put us up for a few more days.

"Thank you very much," I said, "forty-five days is more than I could take. See you on the battlefield in Palestine next time."

Salim went to Homs, Syria, to visit his parents for a short period. I returned briefly to Lebanon and learned that my brother Walid had been beaten up by the Lebanese gendarmes because of my role in the hijacking. Then I left for Amman and resumed my work in Wahdat camp.

# 6 America in Jordan

WHILE MY PERSONAL BATTLE TO FREE THE PALESTINE people had been taking place, the Great Powers had been continuing their attempts to impose their peace solution on the Middle East.

In order to try to implement the UN peace resolution 242, Secretary General U Thant designated Dr. Jarring as his personal representative. The latter set up headquarters in Nicosia, Cyprus, in December 1967. Jarring commuted to Cairo, Beirut, Tel Aviv, and Amman and reported to U Thant on his findings and progress. U Thant made periodic noncommittal reports to the UN, the substance of which was that Dr. Jarring should continue his mission and "pursue" further his efforts to promote "agreement among the parties."

Jarring continued his globe-trotting until April 9, 1969, when his mission was "temporarily suspended" to give more elbow room to the Four Power representatives, as the Israelis put it. The latter were finally reduced to bilateral negotiations under which the United States and the Soviet Union would work out a settlement and decide to "impose" it on both belligerents under UN auspices. The question of denying our existence was moved from the corridors of the UN and multilateral diplomacy to the realm of the great power relations where universal strategic interests preceded our concerns and perhaps even those of the Israelis.

The Arab leadership favored the "imposed solution" because they felt they could more easily justify it on the grounds that they couldn't violate the wishes of the great powers and were not able to resist the whole world single-handedly. Israel felt that these Four Power negotiations were prejudicial. In the first place, Israel had no control over the talks. Secondly, the Israelis felt they were "weighted against Israel" because two powers, namely the Soviet Union and France, were "hostile" to the Israeli position. But all the parties associated with the Middle East conflict intended the year 1969 as the year of solving the "Arab-Israeli conflict" before the guerrillas became too dangerous an alternative to both the Arab regimes and to Israel.

To placate the Palestinians, balloons regarding a

Palestinian entities were floated, and Israel and America looked desperately for credible buyers in the occupied territories and elsewhere. None were available. As the resistance developed into a formidable force and became a magnet to the Arab masses, and as the "impasse" at the UN and Great Power talks intensified, the Four Power discussions were replaced by bilateral negotiations, then by unilateral initiatives, with the Soviets and the Americans continuing to compete publicly for the favors of their respective clients.

It was finally agreed that the US would try to act unilaterally as the mediator with tacit Soviet and Arab approval. With this understanding in mind, the Rogers proposals were put forward on December 9, 1969. Rogers pointed out that "there was an upsurge of hope that a lasting peace would be achieved" after the third Arab-Israeli war in nineteen years. "That hope has unfortunately not been realized," he declared. But because the Middle East "could easily again be the source of another serious conflagration," the US felt it incumbent upon itself to try and avert war by interposing itself as an intermediary to help the parties to the conflict "overcome their legacy of suspicion" and "to achieve a political settlement."

Rogers contended that the US consulted "directly with the Soviet Union, hoping to achieve as wide an area of agreement as possible between us." The decision of the US to act in such a capacity, Rogers said, was made "in full recognition" of four important factors:

1. **First**, we knew that nations not directly involved could not make a durable peace for the peoples and governments involved. Peace rests with the parties to the conflict. The efforts of major powers can help; they can provide a catalyst; they can stimulate the parties to talk; they can encourage; they can help define a realistic framework or agreement; but an agreement among other powers cannot be a substitute for agreement among the parties themselves.
2. **Second**, we knew that a durable peace must meet the legitimate concerns of both sides.
3. **Third**, we were clear that the only framework for a negotiated settlement was one in accordance with the entire text of the UN Security Council resolution. That resolution was agreed upon after long and arduous negotiations; it is carefully balanced; it provides the basis for a just and lasting peace—a final settlement—not merely an interlude between wars.

Fourth, we believed that a protracted period of war, no peace, recurrent violence, and spreading chaos would serve the interests of no nation, in or out of the Middle East.

Rogers appealed to the Arabs "to accept a permanent peace based on a binding agreement," and he urged the Israelis "to withdraw from occupied territory when their territorial integrity is assured as envisaged by the Security Council resolution." He saw the major issues as peace, security, withdrawal, and territory.

To establish a state of peace, belligerency has to be renounced and "conditions and obligations of peace must be specifically defined. Respect for mutual sovereignty and obligations must also be specified." Moreover, Rogers insisted that "a peace agreement between the parties must be based on stated intentions and a willingness to bring about basic changes in the attitudes and conditions which are characteristic of the Middle East today."

To guarantee the peace further, there "should be demilitarized zones and related security arrangements" worked out between the parties with the help of Jarring. Rogers pointed out the need for "secure and recognized boundaries" and suggested that the demarcation line "should not reflect the weight of conquest and should be confined to insubstantial alterations required for mutual security."

On the question of "refugees," he merely acknowledged the fact of the "new consciousness among the young Palestinians" whose aspirations and desires need to be "channeled away from bitterness and frustration toward hope and justice."

Jerusalem, he said, should be a "unified city" with access to all persons, faiths, and nationalities. As to its administration, Rogers proposed "roles for both Israel and Jordan in the civic, economic, and religious life of the city."

On the issue of a separate peace between Israel and Egypt, Rogers admitted that in meetings with the Soviet Union a new formula had been worked out consisting of three principal elements:

1. There should be a binding commitment by Israel and the United Arab Republic to peace with each other.
2. All the specific obligations of peace should be spelled out.
3. The obligation to prevent hostile acts originating from their respective territories should be included.

Second, the detailed provisions of peace relating to security safeguards on the ground should be worked out between the parties, under Ambassador Jarring's auspices. This should utilize the procedures followed in negotiating the armistice agreement under Ralph Bunche in 1949 at Rhodes.

So far as a settlement between Israel and the United Arab Republic goes, these safeguards relate primarily to:

- The area of Sharm el-Sheikh, controlling access to the Gulf of Aqaba

- The need for demilitarized zones as foreseen in the Security Council resolution
- Final arrangements in the Gaza Strip

Third, in the context of peace and agreement on specific security safeguards, the withdrawal of Israeli forces from Egyptian territory would be required.

The Rogers speech aroused concern and suspicion in Israel. Prime Minister Golda Meir denounced the plan as "a grave danger to our very security." Foreign Minister Eban said it "marred prospects for peace." In America, Hubert Humphrey, the presidential hopeful, declared the proposals sacrificed Israel's interests and friendship.

However, a New York Times editorial (December 11, 1969) stated that Rogers' statement was "forthright," sounded "a clear call to reason and fair play," and "honestly pointed the way to a reasonable compromise, the only alternative to a new conflict that neither the nations directly concerned nor the great powers that are perilously involved can afford to risk."

Since Israel dubbed the Rogers proposal as "Arab appeasement," it unleashed the Zionist Movement in America to agitate against the proposals. They aimed to extract concessions from the government or coerce Rogers into retracting on such substantive points as "insubstantial alteration" of borders and a "civic" role for Jordan in Jerusalem. To that end, twenty-four

Zionist organizations in America assembled in Washington on January 25, 1970, ostensibly at the behest of the Conference of Presidents of Major American Jewish Organizations, to express "deep concern and apprehension" over recent US policy statements on the Middle East.

Under this onslaught, Nixon caved in. He not only sent a message to the conference reiterating the American stance of absolute support for Israel, but also dispatched his personal friend and representative, the Zionist Jewish industrialist Max Fisher of Detroit, the chairman of the Council of Jewish Federations and Welfare Fund, to read the message to the Zionists.

Mr. Fisher told the more than one thousand Jewish community and organization leaders that "America stands by its friends. Israel is one of its friends." He went on to say that the president was "prepared to supply military equipment necessary to support the efforts of friendly governments, like Israel's, to defend the safety of their people."

More specifically, the message noted that "the prospects for peace are enhanced as the governments in the area are confident that their borders and their people are secure." Furthermore, the message stressed that peace could only come to the Middle East after "negotiated agreement between Israel and the Arab States."

Dr. William Wexler, chairman of the Conference and president of B'nai B'rith, was disarmed and pleased. He backslid on his "apprehension and concern" and commented: "It [the message] shows that the president understands and shares our concerns. It indicates that he wants no further erosion in American policy."

Wexler concluded by saying that "the Jewish community's disagreement with the State Department was not over motivations or intentions but over tactics."

The Zionists did it again. They got an additional twenty-four Phantom planes to the fifty already delivered in 1968. Rogers was on the defensive, and there was no comparable Arab lobby to counter Zionist power.

Meanwhile, on December 18, 1969, the US "draft" proposal on a "separate peace" between Israel and Jordan, with complete guidelines, was communicated to both parties after consultations with the great powers. In considering the American proposals, one must keep in mind two facts:

1. Syria, whose Golan Heights are under Israeli occupation, is specifically excluded from the big-power discussions.
2. Jordan is under obligation to crush the resistance movement before the proposals are carried out.

Here is a summary of eleven points of the ten-page US document:

**Point 1:**
The parties would determine procedures and a timetable for the withdrawal of Israeli troops from substantially all Jordanian territory occupied in the 1967 war.

**Point 2:**
Each country will accept the obligations of a state of peace between them, including prohibiting any acts of violence from its territory against the other. This would commit Jordan to the prevention of guerrilla raids.

**Point 3:**
The two countries would agree upon a permanent frontier between them, "approximating" to the armistice line before the 1967 war, but allowing for alterations based on practical security requirements and "administrative or economic convenience."

**Point 4:**
Israel and Jordan would settle the problem of ultimate control over Jerusalem, recognizing that the city should be unified, with free traffic through all parts of it, and with both countries sharing in civic and economic responsibilities of city government.

**Point 5:**
Jordan and Israel would participate in working out final arrangements for the administration of the long unsettled Gaza Strip, on the basis of a parallel accord to be reached by Israel and Egypt.

**Point 6:**
The two countries would negotiate practical security arrangements, including the delineation of demilitarized zones on Jordan's West Bank, to take effect with the Israeli withdrawal.

**Point 7:**
Jordan would affirm that the Strait of Tiran and the Gulf of Aqaba are international waterways, open to shipping of all countries, specifically including Israel.

**Point 8:**
This point explains the refugee settlement and notes that the UN's Dr. Gunnar Jarring could establish an international commission to determine the choice of

each refugee on returning to Israel. Since the procedures would undoubtedly be lengthy, the American proposal states that the rest of the package could go into effect before the refugee procedures were carried out.

**Point 9:**
The two countries would enter a mutual agreement formally recognizing each other's sovereignty, territorial integrity, political independence, and right to live in peace.

Point 10:

The total accord would be recorded in a signed document to be deposited with the United Nations. From then on, any breach of any provision could entitle the other country to suspend its obligations until the situation had been corrected.

Point 11:

The completed accord would be "endorsed" by the UN Security Council, and the Big Four powers—Britain, France, the United States, and the Soviet Union—would "concert their future efforts" to help all parties abide by the provisions of the peace.

Finally, the United States notes that an Israeli-Jordanian peace would take effect only with a simultaneous accord between Israel and Egypt, a point stressed by US officials to rebut Arab charges that the peace-making effort is aiming to split the Arab world.

I believe the documentary evidence clearly illustrates America's grand design for the Middle East:

- America looks forward to a permanent Israel, to a neutralized Soviet influence in the area, to continued American predominance, and to a weak and divided Arab world based on personal rivalries and led by military dictatorships or traditional monarchs.
- The proposals submitted by America for the purpose of achieving a "durable peace" postulate a non-Palestinian sovereignty, but America would accede to a Palestinian province under either Jordan or Israel or the joint trusteeship of both.

Denunciations, protestations, charges, and counter-charges against these proposals by Arab governments, Israel, or the Soviet Union were, in my judgment, just part of the overall deception on the part of the participants to carry out the proposals at the expense of the Arab masses in general and the Palestinian people in particular.

The problem remained of how Egypt and Israel would view the arrangement and each maintain its presumed "superiority" and how the superpowers would respond to the demand of their client. It is true that an all-out conflict in the region could "drag" in the great powers, but if both have a priori accord not to intervene and to confront each other at the regional level, then whatever struggle is waged by mistake or calculation would not escalate into an all-engulfing war.

Therefore, there is ample room for maneuvering by all concerned. It is only in this context that Israel's attempt to topple Nasser in the autumn of 1969 and winter of 1970 can be understood. The great powers supposedly counseled restraint, but the Israelis were bent on overthrowing Nasser as the only obstacle to the kind of "peace" they desired.

Finally, the Russians supported Egypt with missiles, which forced the Israelis to cease their deep penetration forays into Egypt, but handed them a big propaganda stick to beat the Americans with and demand that the Russian weaponry be matched in order to maintain the "balance of power" in favor of Israel.

Americans, never bashful about endorsing Zionism and its claims, joined a well-orchestrated, worldwide Zionist campaign. This campaign argued that thousands of Soviet technicians and pilots had taken over everything in Egypt's military apparatus, from military training to manning the Sam missiles to flying combat missions against the Israelis. Moreover, the latter let it be known that they were prepared to take on the Russians and their Arab allies.

But the Soviets not only refused to provide Egypt with the needed offensive capability to liberate the occupied territories but declined to supply her with adequate defensive capability with which to safeguard the ridiculous static positions the Egyptians maintained in the open desert on the advice of the Russians.

As to the contention that the Egyptians were preparing an amphibious assault to cross the Suez Canal, it turned out to be a propaganda hoax concocted by the State Department and the Zionists to justify more American military and economic aid to Israel. At no time did the Egyptians ever constitute a threat to Israeli air power or contemplate crossing the Canal. All they sought was the limited objective of preventing the Israelis from roaming UAR skies at will.

This, of course, didn't please Moshe Dayan and his American sponsors. Nasser's entire strategy was based on the retention of power, not the liberation of occupied territory, as his so-called "war of attrition" advocates proclaimed so vociferously. But surprisingly enough, he always stated that Palestine could only be liberated by force of arms. He nevertheless was reconciled to a Zionist-controlled Palestine based on June 4, 1967, borders. As a proponent of the "political solution," he never deviated from that stance, except to make periodic bombastic speeches for Arab home consumption.

Thus, while diplomats held secret sessions, chancelleries exchanged aide-mémoires, and foreign ministers roved the world in search of peace "based on justice," Hussein, as a sign of goodwill towards his Western friends, moved to the implementation phase of the Rogers proposals regarding an Israeli-Jordanian peace: the planned elimination of the resistance.

While these political machinations were going on, I was on a three-month tour of the Arab Gulf and Iraq with a team of revolutionary stalwarts:

- Salah Salah, the Palestinian labor leader and graduate of Syrian prisons for his Pan-Arabist political work
- Rashida Obeida, the much-feared female underground fighter from the occupied territories
- Salim Issawi of TWA fame

- Talaat, the revolutionary who for thirteen years had terrorized the Zionists of Europe

The purpose of the tour was to spread revolutionary propaganda as well as collect funds for the Front. It was a tremendous success. We not only reached and communicated with the Arab masses, but we learned a good deal about their concerns, especially their desire to oust the British from the Arab Gulf and to stop encroaching Yankee neocolonialism in the area.

It was the poor, the workers, and peasants who received us and showered us with gifts, not the oil kings or the political advisers of the local "bandits." We returned to Amman in early February, to the vortex of counter-revolutionary conspiracy.

King Hussein had just arrived from Cairo after extensive consultation with the front-line states. He appeared to be in a belligerent state of mind as he made some strong statements threatening dire consequences if the Israelis did not carry out Resolution 242. Yet, he immediately promulgated several restrictive decrees which, in effect, banished the resistance from the cities, closed down its newspapers, and banned its public assemblies. A showdown was inevitable.

First of all, we decided to break the siege that Hussein had imposed on the cities. Each sector of the resistance took the necessary countermeasures. I was assigned to go to Schular Camp near Zarqa to give public lectures against Hussein's decrees and to explain to our masses that Hussein's actions could not be separated from those of the US and Israel. Other comrades carried the Front's political line to all the camps in Jordan. Hussein retaliated by shutting off the camps' water and electricity—a deed he was going to repeat in September with devastating effects on the poor.

We challenged his position and called for demonstrations throughout Jordan. His goons tried to disrupt our public meetings and stir up riots, but most of them met revolutionary justice. Tension was rapidly mounting as I returned to Amman and was ordered to go and give another public lecture at Jabel Al-Taj school. When I arrived with a few comrades, we discovered that the audience had been dispersed by Hussein's troops and the air bristled with the sound of machine guns. The Front's local commander advised us to go back to Wahdat camp until further notice. We did so without question.

On the eve of February 10, I was saddled with the presence of my fiancé's sister, Samirah, who had just come from Baghdad to visit Bassim and ascertain for the family if I were worthy of becoming their daughter-in-law. Bassim and I had gotten engaged earlier with the approval of the Front. Neither family was consulted before the announcement. Samirah had had no military training, and I had no place to keep her at a safe distance from the battlefront. I was worried about her.

In a blunt Iraqi manner, she eased my fears: "Leila, I will do whatever you ask of me. I, too, am an Arab, and I want to fight." Happily, I said, "All right, come with me to Jabel Amman to deliver some messages."

I picked up a gun and a hand grenade and took a taxi. As we climbed uphill, we saw a burning military jeep and heard exchanges of gunfire. Some brothers from Fateh stopped us and warned us it was too dangerous to go any further.

The driver ordered us out of his taxi, saying he wasn't ready to die. I tried to persuade him to continue, but he didn't yield. Samirah was infuriated and denounced him as a shameless coward. The poor fellow said he had eight children to support and left us after refusing to accept the fare. The brothers from Fateh reported that the whole area was aflame and people were being evacuated.

One of them recognized me and said the battle had already started, "Get back to Wahdat camp, Leila." I showed him the grenade and assured him I was ready to fight. He grinned and said, "Come with me, let's phone the military bureau and tell them that all signs indicate that Hussein is about to launch a murderous attack against us." We did. Then Samirah and I returned to Wahdat camp to report on developments.

Upon our arrival, Dr. Habash ordered us to prepare petrol bombs to use against Hussein's soldiers. I went to the nearest petrol station to purchase some petrol. The attendant said I could have all the petrol I wanted and refused to accept a single fils for it. We spent practically the whole night making bombs and distributing them among our guerrillas. Since the Front had no weapons supplier, we had to rely on our own resources and on weapons we captured from the enemy.

Comrade Nadia, a lady squad commander recently appointed to the region, discovered that we were low on ammunition and weapons. Without informing anyone, she led her squad in five military operations on Jordanian police stations, netting over eighty weapons and hundreds of rounds of ammunition without a single casualty.

At midnight, comrade Soulafah and I volunteered to go to Jabel Amman to inspect our positions and get first-hand reports on Hussein's moves. The leadership agreed, on the condition that we traveled in civilian clothes. Before we left, however, we insisted that Dr. Habash be placed in a more secure place, elsewhere in Amman. He objected strongly, "Why should I live if you, Soulafah, and Leila, are prepared to die for the cause?"

We left silently and returned to Wahdat camp very late that night. No sooner had we fallen asleep than we were awakened by the music of sub-machine guns and the roar of Hussein's artillery. Each fighter immediately assumed his or her assigned task. I had to go to the mosque with comrade Waddad to start broadcasting the battlefield news and urge our masses to rally to the defense of the revolution.

February 10, 1970, was the first massive attack on the resistance since November of 1968. The battle raged on all day, but Hussein's troops were unable to break through our impregnable positions. Amman was under fire from all directions, but the resistance stood up to Hussein fearlessly, and he was forced to back down after the first full day of fighting. Sporadic fighting continued for about a week, however, and hundreds of people were killed and maimed. The resistance sustained a number of grievous losses.

The Front suffered the loss of Abu Talaat, one of our most courageous commanders. Abu Talaat's assassination by Hussein intelligence services saddened the whole resistance movement and strengthened our resolve to fight against the Hashemite despot. Abu Talaat was given a hero's funeral. Thousands accompanied his cortege to the cemetery. As we bid him goodbye, Ramzia, wife of Abdul Mohsen Hassan, a martyr killed by the Israelis in Zurich, Switzerland, delivered a brief, moving oration without shedding a tear:

"Abu Talaat, you live. Three children survive you. Abdul Mohsen left me with nine. Both of you left twelve guerrillas for Palestine to carry on the torch of her freedom. I assure you we shall recover the land for which you died at the hands of dastardly criminals. Fallen hero, we salute you. You died in battle wearing your boots. You set an example to the Palestinians and all oppressed everywhere."

May your kind multiply a thousandfold. Embrace the earth whence you came and melt into the eternity of Palestine so that her soil may be further nourished by the blood of martyrs and heroes. You live because the revolution will live.

Hussein's barbaric onslaught against the resistance forced its various contingents to make a preliminary attempt at unifying its ranks. Thus, the Unified Command was born in the midst of streams of blood and under the chains of Hussein's US-supplied tanks.

However, no concrete revolutionary strategy was agreed upon, and no united action was attempted, although many comrades were killed or wounded because of the lack of concerted action. By May 6, the resistance nominally adopted the strategy of the Front to stave off the multilateral plot that was being engineered to destroy the resistance.

Meanwhile, Hussein saw the writing on the wall. He rescinded his decrees in a "magnanimous" gesture of "Arab solidarity" and explained the reaction of the resistance to his decree as "a misunderstanding." His Western apologists explained Hussein's "statesmanship" as a means to avert a civil war, "to head off a bloodbath," because he did not want to be "a hated prisoner in his palace," and because "It does not seem in Hussein's character, nor to be in his concept of kingship, to contemplate such a state of affairs" (London Observer, February 17, 1970). Nevertheless, it was admitted that Hussein had been urged for months by the US embassy in Amman to "have it out" with the Palestinians.

In February 1970, the subterranean currents in Jordan became clear to even the casual observer. Unfortunately, many intelligent people refused to believe their eyes, let alone take any action. The two irreconcilable forces that held dual authority in Amman indeed had to "have it out." The question was when? Hussein deferred a showdown for two reasons.

First, Fateh and generally the Arab masses still believed in the myth of Arab brotherhood and were prepared to co-exist with him. Second, he still regarded the resistance as a valuable tool with which to bludgeon the United States and Israel to obtain more concessions for the time being and a more favorable peace accord when the time came.

Intermittent fighting occurred between the resistance and American henchmen in Amman. Joseph Sisco, the

Assistant Secretary for Middle Eastern Affairs, visited Jordan in mid-April. The masses gave a thunderous "No" to America's "peace" plans. But neither America nor Hussein was prepared to relent. The well-planned conspiracy was slowly unfolding as Hussein's special security squads (SSS) roamed the streets of major cities and provoked the resistance. As the Arab front-line states inched closer to "peace" with Israel, their media focused on the shortcomings of the resistance.

Jordan's hirelings were openly flouting Jordanian laws, causing chaos and trying to provoke a civil war between Palestinians and Jordanians. The Popular Front for the Liberation of Palestine foresaw the implications of such a policy, which exploited the major weakness of the resistance—a weakness brought about by Fateh's right-wing leadership—and immediately launched a counteroffensive calling on all citizens to unite under one banner.

The PF seized the initiative by capturing strategic areas in Amman and took the First Secretary of the American embassy as a hostage to isolate and expose the corrupt elements that stood behind Hussein and his CIA "advisers." Under pressure from the resistance, we released him, but the counterrevolutionary violence intensified rather than diminished, contrary to the resistance's expectations.

The PF moved in and occupied the Philadelphia and Intercontinental Hotels and took all foreigners hostage. Hussein was savagely shelling the camps of "his subjects" under the pretext that an assassination attempt had been made on his life, but stopped when he discovered we meant business. Fighting raged for a week. More than one thousand people were sacrificed in honor of Hussein's throne, yet by an ironic twist of fate, a cease-fire was arranged, and joint committees representing Hussein and the guerrillas were set up to supervise the "truce."

The massacre, in the best American tradition of explaining conspiracies away, was finally blamed on the anger of a single, isolated person, General Zeid Bin Shaker, whose sister was allegedly killed by a guerrilla prior to the start of fighting. Both he and Sharif Nassir, the uncle of Hussein, "resigned" their generalships, and Hussein assumed sole command of "his" armed forces.

The events of June showed that Fateh had not learned its lesson. We missed the opportunity to depose Hussein when we had the confidence of the people and the power to defeat his fragmented forces. Between June and September, Hussein consolidated his forces, purged wavering elements, and eliminated all potentially disloyal Palestinians in the higher echelons of his armed forces.

Fateh, as "the largest" commando organization, was faltering and vacillating. During June, it became clear to all that the "backbone" of the resistance was not leading but following the masses. The Popular Front, needless to say, took the initiative and forced the other groups in the resistance to follow its lead. Well-thought-out strategy and imaginative leadership held sway.

The Popular Front was progressively becoming the new alternative, the new magnet of the oppressed, the vanguard of the Arab social revolution. Arab "reactionary" and "progressive" regimes began to distinguish between "honest" revolutionaries (Fateh) and "terrorist" revolutionaries with "imported ideologies" (the Popular Front). Hussein insolently declared that it was the Front's behavior, not his criminal bombardment of defenseless "refugee" camps, that shamed the Arab people.

The masses were not deceived; they knew who the enemy was and applauded our action when we valiantly defended our fortresses in the camps with courage and without compromise at the negotiation table. The Front and its deeds became synonymous. Everyone knew we were deadly serious revolutionaries, not "revolutionaries" seeking a "peaceful, political solution" by diplomatic means and using the fighting as a sideshow to demonstrate that we could cause trouble.

The masses were for liberation, not capitulation; they rallied behind their Front as the exponent of the doctrine of people's war and protracted armed struggle. The line of demarcation between the enemy and the friend of the people became even sharper in the spring of 1970. The masses knew that Hussein and the Arab reactionaries were an integral part of the enemy camp.

What the masses had been indoctrinated into believing was that the Arab "progressives" stood for liberation and the nationalist, pan-Arabist wave of the revolution—a wave that challenged imperialism, Zionism, and Arab reaction. In that fateful spring, the "progressives" unmasked themselves as they emitted "peace" gestures to Washington and Tel Aviv, with Moscow's approval. By September 1970, their "peace" strategy and attempts to liquidate the resistance were clearly evident. By July 1971, they became abundantly clear as Sadat ditched Nasserism and unleashed "a war of attrition" against the Popular Front from the august halls of Cairo University.

In his May Day 1970 speech, Nasser stated that the opportunity for an Arab-American rapprochement was rapidly fading. Instead of the usual abuse directed against the United States, he said that America was one-sided and biased in favor of Israel. Then Nasser invited America to repair its relations with the Arabs on the basis of Scranton's "evenhandedness" of December 1968—clearly an invitation to America, the Zionists' accomplice, to act as an intermediary in the Arab-Israeli conflict. Nasser thought he was putting America on the defensive; he was in for a surprise when Rogers answered him affirmatively on June 19.

Rogers resuscitated the old doctrine of "peace based on justice." Diplomatic flirtation was carried on for a month. Then came Nasser's historic bombshell: on July 23, 1970, on the eighteenth anniversary of the revolution, he accepted the Rogers proposals for peace in the Middle East. Nasser agreed not just to "peace" with Israel as a long-term objective, but also to the cessation of the "war of attrition," an "arms freeze," and Israel's non-withdrawal from occupied territories prior to negotiations. Nasser's "brilliant diplomatic tactic," as his confidant, Mohammed Hassanein Heikal, labeled it, sent a shock wave through Arab revolutionary ranks.

The "contradictions" of Zionist society, as Nasser had foreseen, came to the open; Gahel, the right-wing party, quit the "national coalition" when Israel accepted the cease-fire. The Arab states, with the exception of Iraq and Algeria, gave verbal support to Nasser's "peace offensive."

Journalists hailed Nasser's statesmanship. The Palestinians, the worshippers of Nasser in Amman and in occupied Jerusalem and major West Bank cities, went through the streets shouting: "Nasser is a coward; Nasser is a traitor." Nasser's image was tarnished, but he remained the idol of the masses.

However, when he expelled Palestinian students from Egyptian universities, closed down Fateh's broadcasting station, and ordered his allies in the resistance to support his position publicly and to try to eliminate the Popular Front, Nasser's stock plummeted. If he was not completely exposed as a Yankee collaborator, his actions created gnawing doubts in the minds of his erstwhile admirers.

The die was cast.

The revolutionary embryo was alone; the Russians, the Yankees, the Arab ruling cliques, and the Zionists were united for the purpose of aborting the fetus of hope.

In his July 23 speech, President Nasser proclaimed Egypt's aims: Israeli withdrawal from all occupied Arab territory and recognition of the legitimate rights of the Palestinian people.

"We do not want war for war's sake," he said. "We want to liberate our land; we want the rights of the Palestinian people. We have accepted the American proposals presented by Secretary of State William Rogers; we do not see anything new in them; we have accepted them in the past. It is Israel who rejects them. Israel drops one thousand tons of bombs on us. Yet, when modern Soviet weapons arrived in Egypt, a full attack was made, and no American newspaper mentioned that Israel has seventy-two missile bases for defense. What does this mean? Does it mean we have no right to defend ourselves when Israel has such a right, and a right to attack us?"

The crucial implication of Nasser's stance—the destruction of the resistance movement as a precondition to peace—was not admitted. Nasser insisted that Egypt had a right to sue for peace and the Palestinians had a right to fight for the liberation of their country: two contradictory rights.

Nasser's decision to accept the Rogers proposals had a demoralizing effect on the Arab world and a devastating impact on the resistance, notwithstanding Al-Ahram reports to the contrary. Within two weeks of the ill-conceived pronouncement, a "cease-fire" order was issued and began on August 7, 1970. The expected coexistence between Zionist and Arab did not materialize.

The resistance was the main obstacle; it had to be crushed before the elder statesmen of Zionism and Arabism marched hand in hand to the altar of Solomon's temple and Omar's mosque.

Joint efforts to contain the resistance were mounted:

- Funds stopped pouring into Fateh's coffers.
- A worldwide propaganda war against the resistance was declared.
- The movement of resistance groups across frontiers was carefully monitored and gravely curtailed in strategic areas within Jordan.

Hussein, with Arab silence—therefore, approval—immediately launched his systematic liquidation campaign against "honest and terroristic" revolutionaries without distinction.

It was hoped that this latest campaign would be the final assault before the reign of peace descended on the Middle East.

The Front waited long enough to let every Arab leader, every friend and foe, show his hand. Some Arab leaders denounced Hussein's policies; others silently wrung their hands; most applauded his stand on "law and order." Then the Front decided to implement its offensive strategy. The resistance as a whole should have taken the offensive, but it didn't.

My comrades and I were on our way to Europe to declare international war against the concerted attempts of the superpowers, Zionism, and the Arab states to smash the Arab social revolution and thereby the revolution of the Third World and the oppressed everywhere on this globe.

I went to Frankfurt in the full knowledge that we, the Palestinians, the children of despair and now of revolution, were carrying the torch of freedom and human liberation on behalf of humanity. If we failed, America would have succeeded in reversing the tide of the world revolution, with the notable exception of Vietnam.

Our minimum objective was the inscription of the name of Palestine on the memory of mankind and on the mind of every self-respecting libertarian who believes in the right of the subjugated to self-determination. Furthermore, we hoped to arrest the Fascist terror in Jordan and reveal the contradictions of Arab society. We were out to strike at the heart of the oppressor.

# 7 We Speak for a Lost Humanity

The Popular Front, in its manifold institutions, is a miniature of the Arab world we hope to build. Each member must therefore learn to serve the common good and do his utmost to help the Front attain the liberation of the Arab man and his Zionist foe.

**George El-Bekaai**

## The Principal Functions of Every Member in the Popular Front

The principal functions are:

- Politically oriented military activities
- Spreading revolutionary propaganda
- Fund-raising

While these functions are often closely associated, each comrade specializes in the area to which his or her talents are best suited. However, the party requires that each one of us:

- Has a good grasp of the ideology and strategy
- Be prepared to undertake military operations in the occupied territories or in foreign lands

- Always be willing to live and work with the masses
- Help collect funds in a variety of ways, from selling the Front's theoretical journal, *Al-Hadaf*, to raising money from European and American friends and supporters

In my capacity as a soldier, I was selected to carry out foreign operations. Unfortunately, my identity had been revealed by the Syrian authorities in 1969 when comrade Salim Issawi and I landed the TWA 840 in Damascus. If the Syrians had not interfered, I would have remained one of the hundreds of anonymous soldiers at the Front.

Thanks to Zionist hysteria, my name and photograph have probably appeared in every paper in the West, if not the entire world. But the wide publicity did not prove an effective means of ending my career as a revolutionary. I was not out of the picture yet.

While many members of the Front thought that I was working in Irbid in the spring and summer of 1970, and my family thought that I was still in Egypt, I was, in fact, training to commandeer an El-Al plane. Details of the training must still remain secret.

After the first hijacking, I was elected to the central committee of the Front, a position that has not diminished but increased my obligations. In the Front, the higher one ascends in its organizational hierarchy, the more responsibilities one has to assume. There are none of those celebrities in the Front who perform innocuous bureaucratic functions and are surrounded by kowtowing assistants.

In early March 1970, I left Amman for an undisclosed destination where I underwent three plastic surgery operations so that I could continue our planned military operations. It was difficult at first to find a doctor ready to put his medicine at the service of the revolution. After extensive searches, a physician was found who was anxious to help, but he couldn't understand why a prospective husband would want to see his wife's face "disfigured" before he'd marry her.

"He must be nuts," the good doctor insisted.

"Nuts," we agreed, but "Please operate," we said.

The doctor shook his head, booked an obstetrics hospital, and reached for his "syslestics." It was March 13, 1970, when the first "face-twisting" was performed. It was extremely painful. Since I refused a general anesthetic, I could see as well as feel the thrust of the needles. I suppose people in the West will conclude that I must be a masochist, but I assure them that I am not: I have a cause higher and nobler than my own, a cause to which all private interests and concerns must be subordinated. Here then I lay on the operating table while my comrades were being tortured, my sisters being raped, and my land pillaged.

For twenty days after the first operation, I had to live on liquids. I felt terribly weak. Since the operation was a secret which less than a half dozen people knew about, I languished in the hospital with no visitors to break the boredom. I spent my days watching the comings and goings in the maternity ward across the hall. To complicate matters, my nurse spoke neither Arabic nor English. She was Armenian, and we could communicate only by sign language, a situation which didn't help my painful face.

Happily, no one in the hospital recognized me. But one day, when I was calling for a nurse, a man who was visiting his wife in the room next door walked in to help. He recognized me and called me by my first name. I denied that I was Leila. He didn't believe me. When I left the hospital, I gave his new daughter a necklace made of bullets and wished her a long, long revolutionary career.

Zero hour was approaching rapidly, yet more surgery was required to complete my "beauty treatment." Two more operations were performed, the last a few days before the scheduled hijacking. Most of my comrades were already in Europe waiting to meet me. Suddenly, word came through that everything must be postponed to avoid confrontation with Jordan. I was a little disappointed but not disheartened.

The Israelis and their allies, however, were a vigilant and sleepless enemy. I had been released from the hospital. It was July 11, 1970, at two fifteen a.m., and I was sitting in Dr. Wadi Haddad's apartment, and we were discussing strategy. His wife and child were asleep in the next room. From out of nowhere, a volley of rockets struck the bedroom. Neither of us was hurt. We reached for our guns. Then, in the midst of flames, his family burst out of the bedroom screaming and bleeding. The electricity failed. We panicked momentarily as we tried to extinguish the fire. I grabbed eight-year-old Hani and ran up and down the stairs shouting, "Fire, fire."

Hani was bleeding from the chest, and his feet looked squashed. A neighbor invited us to take refuge in her apartment and called the fire brigade. I was anxious, but Hani was absolutely calm and silent. He forced a smile and said to me, "Leila, revolutionaries of the Front ought not to be fearful. You ought to be ashamed to be frightened." I was a little shocked by the reminder from this child revolutionary, and I pounced on him and carried him outside to take him to the hospital. I stopped a cabby, who refused to transport us, and I spat in his face.

Suddenly, Abu Dardock, a member of the Front, appeared on the scene, and away we went to the American University Hospital's emergency ward. As I rushed in with Hani in my arms, blood covering both of us, I cried, "Find me a doctor, please."

Within minutes, a doctor was there, but before he even looked at the child, he callously inquired if I had the money to pay for the treatment. I shrieked at him, "Are you a doctor or a carpet salesman?" He firmly explained that AUB was a "hospital, not a charity center."

"Since you are in business, take me for ransom, but please look after the child," I begged. At that moment, Dr. Haddad and his wife stormed in looking for their child. His mother was almost hysterical. The American doctor recognized Dr. Haddad, a fellow MD, and was taken aback, apologizing profusely. His apologies fell on deaf ears. I voiced my threats loudly, "Yankee doctor, the revolution will make AUB's hospital a hospital for the poor, and your kind of doctor will have to be disbarred or sent back to America." He flashed a barefaced grin and said, "I'm sorry."

The attack on Dr. Haddad's apartment strengthened our resolve to fight the enemy with all the power at our command. We were much more determined to die for the cause than ever before. The sight of the apartment in flames was constantly on my mind as I flew to Frankfurt in August.

In Frankfurt, I stayed at a moderately priced hotel whose owner turned out to be Jewish. He greeted me in Arabic, and I hesitated momentarily before replying, then casually reciprocated his greeting, pretending that I was a non-Arab. He persisted in talking Arabic to me and boastfully announced, "I am a Jew, you know."

I promptly replied, "I am an Arab, and I am not against the Jews; I am against the Zionists and the people who occupied Arab territory."

He countered agreeably, "I am a Zionist for religious reasons, but I am not interested in politics." After our confrontation ended, I went upstairs to my room and stayed put until the following morning. Finally, I became restless and hungry and decided to go out to eat and take a long walk.

My Jewish friend was at the desk. He greeted me volubly and asked if I would like to go to Amsterdam on a trip he was organizing for his guests. I smiled, declined the invitation, and rushed out to fetch some food.

On the way, I purchased several English newspapers; all were filled with news from Jordan, and some had editorial comments on the impact of the Rogers proposals on the Arab world, Israel, and great power relations. Practically every paper I read speculated on forthcoming hijackings. I felt uneasy at first, but then relieved when I read that the hijackings were supposed to be taking place in Zurich and elsewhere, not in Amsterdam.

I was obsessed with the idea of my mission. I rehearsed it on the hour, every hour of my waking days. I roamed the city of Frankfurt for a few days, bored with the waiting; then I went to Stuttgart briefly and on to Amsterdam. Our rendezvous with history was approaching: all plans had to be translated into action; history was ours to write; Patrick Arguello was to write it in blood; I was not so honored.

I met Patrick Arguello for the first time in September 1970, in front of the air terminal at Stuttgart. We briefed each other on our mutual assignment and reviewed the plan thoroughly. The following day, we flew together to Frankfurt. At Frankfurt airport, Mr. Diaz (Patrick) was inspected as I watched the passengers of a TWA Tel Aviv-bound flight being thoroughly searched. I felt very happy that we were causing the enemy so much trouble.

"What fools, that's the plane we're going to hijack on its way back from Tel Aviv," I thought to myself. Patrick was cleared through customs without suspicion. The next stop was Amsterdam.

On September 6, Patrick and I met in front of the El-Al counter at ten a.m. We waited for half an hour for the El-Al office to open. It never opened that day. We checked the flight schedule; the bulletin board still showed El-Al flight 219 as departing for New York at eleven twenty a.m. We asked the KLM ground hostess for assistance. She took our tickets and called the El-Al office. There was no answer.

The KLM hostess seemed a little surprised. She asked, "Why take El-Al flight? There are others that are better and more comfortable." We assured her that "we'd rather travel El-Al."

As we waited, Pan Am flight 840 arrived, and I happily remembered TWA flight 840 of August 29, 1969. I was not aware at that moment that two of our comrades, having been barred in an earlier attempt by the Israelis, were on their own to seize Pan Am flight 840 a half-hour after takeoff. They took the 747 to Cairo, where they blew it up as a declaration of Palestinian independence.

Neither Patrick nor any of the other five male hijackers knew that three planes were our target that day. Only the three female Palestinian captains and a handful of other leaders knew of the entire plan.

We lingered in the waiting room until about twelve o'five. There was still no sign of the El-Al counter staff. Suddenly, an armed police officer in Israeli uniform emerged.

"Why are you late?" he demanded.

I accommodatingly explained, "We arrived at ten o'clock, officer," and suggested that he ask the KLM hostess, who vouched for us.

"Your passport, please," he said. Both Patrick and I showed him our passports without comment. The officer carefully examined each page. He looked at my photograph and then back at me several times. He paced back and forth as he addressed us. He asked me to empty my handbag and identify every item in it, which I did.

I looked completely normal. Patrick was wearing a business suit, and I was dressed in a mini-skirt and jacket. I did not pretend to be other than calm Maria Sanchez from Honduras. Routine questions went on for several minutes.

Suddenly, I heard loud voices. I saw three Arabs walking in my direction. My heart sank. I knew and recognized one of them. What if he greeted me? We would be exposed immediately.

Fortunately, the Israeli officer had his back to them. Since we were already holding hands for his benefit, I quickly threw my arms around Patrick. He seemed a little surprised, but what man will rebuff a woman under such conditions?

The embrace lasted until my Arab friend passed by, unnoticed by the El-Al officer or anyone else. The officer seemed untroubled by us and politely invited us to go with him to the basement to check our baggage.

"Officer, our luggage is open; you could inspect it anytime you like," I said.

"Regulations state, Madam," he explained, "that owners must be present."

We happily agreed. The officer was no amateur. He systematically went through every item not once, but twice. He asked informal but pertinent questions as he inspected our possessions.

Then he pointedly turned to me and asked, "Has anyone given you any gifts?"

"No," I replied emphatically.

"Do you have anything sharp or dangerous?"

"Such as?" I said.

"Such as a pistol, a knife, or anything sharp?"

"No, Sir. What would a girl like me ever do with a pistol or knife, officer?"

He smiled apologetically and said, "You can go back to the transit hall."

Then it suddenly dawned on him to ask me in English if I spoke Spanish.

"Sí, señor," I blurted out boldly.

"Have a good journey," he said.

Patrick was a little surprised. "Why would you say to him you spoke Spanish when you don't?"

"Look, Patrick," I said, "if he knew how to speak Spanish, he would have addressed us in Spanish from the beginning. Calm down, we're clear."

As we re-entered the hall, I saw some thirty or forty youngsters waiting to board El-Al flight 219. I was shocked and secretly lamented that once again I had to face the agonizing problem of what to do to avoid hurting children. I love children, and I know they are free from guilt. Although I remembered the children of Palestine napalmed by the Israelis and Dr. Haddad's child running out of his flaming room, I nevertheless vowed to do my utmost not to jeopardize the lives of the passengers needlessly. I sat semi-paralyzed for a few seconds, wrestling with the moral issues of our action.

Meanwhile, Patrick was walking around the hall trying to spot our two comrades. As I looked at the children, a beautiful little girl walked towards me, her eyes directed longingly towards the sandwich in my hand. Her mother pulled her away as I almost said to her, "Taali ela houna." (Come here and take it.) No sooner did I hold my tongue than her mother called "Taali ela houna ya binti," (Come here my child). I was startled. Patrick had just joined me.

I tried to dispel any sign of anxiety by whispering furtively to him, "Guess what?"

"Yes," said Patrick, thinking I had spotted our comrades.

"The lady with the children opposite us is an Israeli; imagine if she were assigned to hijack this plane and she wanted to take it in one direction and we in the other. Who is likely to win the contest?" I asked.

Patrick laughed and assured me, "We shall win."

We waited. Minutes seemed like hours. No Israeli plane was in sight. Only the damned KLM planes were there, and we had no use for them. The jumbo jet had taken off at eleven-thirty. It was now a little after twelve. The Israeli officer reappeared, and we went through the same routine inspection.

We were ordered to another side of the room. I tried not to show my frustration. The third inspection started, and we were told to move back to our original places. By the end of this inspection, it was one-thirty. The hijack proclamations were supposed to have been simultaneously announced at twelve-twenty. I figured that either the hijackings were announced and the blasted Israelis had heard about them and decided to transfer us to KLM, or they had captured our two other comrades and were desperately looking for us.

I had two hand grenades; Patrick had one hand grenade and a pistol. I said to Patrick, who was aware only of our own hijack plans, "Commandos do not surrender; we have to play Samson if they discover us." Patrick resolutely agreed.

We were asked to walk downstairs. The same officer was standing at the gate, checking every passport and passenger. I said, "Officer, we are late." "That's all right, madam, we're doing it for your own security," he declared. We marched to the plane surrounded by all kinds of armed guards. I was delighted that the resistance was causing so many difficulties and making the Zionists paranoid and jittery. I felt that Patrick and I had already conquered the enemy and accomplished half of our mission by making a fool of him and proving that his precautionary measures were not foolproof. I realized that the enemy's fortress was not impregnable as I ascended the plane with twelve guards of honor bearing sub-machine guns guaranteeing my "security."

When I stepped into the El-Al plane, I felt for the first time since April 13, 1948, that I was at home again in Haifa. I was indeed in a lion's den. Never before had I felt so elated and proud of being a member of the Popular Front than at that moment.

Patrick and I searched for two empty seats. We were moved around twice until we were finally seated together in the second row of the tourist class. We heaved a sigh of relief as a hostess asked if we were comfortable. I was exhilarated and looked forward to the second half of our mission.

Patrick seemed a little frightened as El-Al finally took off around one-thirty. Patrick knew me only as Shadiah. I thought if I revealed my identity, his morale would be greatly boosted. I did. Patrick was heartened and gave me a victory salute. The lady next to me fell asleep immediately. All the passengers seemed tired.

At one-fifty-five, we noticed that someone was watching us from the back of the plane. I told Patrick to stay still. I turned around and looked directly at the man for a minute. He was in civilian clothes. When he saw that I was watching him, he shyly looked the other way.

At that moment, Patrick prepared his hand grenade and pistol. I pulled the safety pins off my two hand grenades and rushed forward through the first-class section towards the cockpit. We shouted, "Don't move," as some of the passengers tried to take cover.

Three stewards were in front of us wielding handguns. In a couple of seconds, I could count six guns. But we had anticipated a battle. A hostess fell to the ground, crying to me in Arabic. I threatened to blow up the plane if anyone fired at us. I displayed my two grenades and dropped the safety pins on the floor, hoping to convince everyone we intended business and to avert a bloody battle.

Patrick held the armed stewards and the passengers at bay. "Go ahead, I'll protect your back," he instructed me. I forced the hostess to stand up and walk ahead of me. The moment she opened the door, she staggered forward in a state of panic.

I couldn't see the captain or crew. Shots were fired. There was another door before we could reach the pilot's cabin. Both of us banged on the door. No one opened the door. Suddenly, someone was looking at us through a spyhole. I brandished my hand grenades and ordered him to open the door or else.

I heard more shots, and the plane went into a spin. Several people attacked me at the same moment. I thought the plane was disintegrating. The firing continued, and suddenly I found myself besieged by a pack of wolves: El-Al staff as well as passengers. Someone screamed, "Don't shoot at her! She has two hand grenades." No one fired at me, but some people were kicking me, others hitting me. A few just stepped all over me. Two were holding my hands and trying to take away the grenades. One finally succeeded in prying one grenade from me without exploding himself and the plane. I held tightly to the other until I was knocked unconscious for a second and was overpowered.

At first, I didn't know what was happening to Patrick. Within a few minutes, I was dragged to the first-class compartment where Patrick was lying, bleeding profusely and breathing heavily. I could see he was still alive.

The Zionists were acting like mad dogs. They trampled over every part of our bodies. By that time, Patrick was too weak to resist. I was fighting like a caged lion. I fought until I was completely exhausted. Then a vicious thug pounced on me, pulled my hair mercilessly, and called me a wicked bitch, a malicious Arab, and all sorts of obscene names. I spat contemptuously in his face. I bit his hands. He and the others around me beat me incessantly for several minutes.

The plane was traveling smoothly; the remaining passengers were staying in their seats. Suddenly, an Israeli guard emerged from the cockpit area. Patrick was lying on his side. The man turned him over on his stomach and started tying him up with wires and a necktie.

Someone asked, "How are they?"

A voice replied, "We don't know. He is... we're not sure. She's three quarters dead."

The man stepped on Patrick's hips, and Patrick looked at me in agony, his hands tied behind his back. Then the Zionist guard fired four shots into Patrick's back. Someone screamed from the back of the plane, "Please stop the bloodshed. Please, please, please!" The four shots that were fired into Patrick's back were fired from a distance of less than one foot. Patrick looked at me, gave me a deathly smile, and bid me an eternal goodbye.

Then came my turn. I was tied up in the same fashion: hands behind my back, my feet and legs immobilized with wires. I expected to join the ranks of our martyrs as Patrick had just done. But the Zionists did not execute me. I was certain they were not moved by any humanitarian concern or by the pleading voice from the back of the cabin. They needed me for display purposes in their human zoo in Israel. I presumed they wanted a witness to testify to their "bravery" - a prisoner to torture and to extract confessions from.

As they finished tying me up, the pilot announced, "We are going to Tel Aviv."

Yet within minutes, I felt the plane descend and then touch down. As it hit the runway, I fell off my seat and my "bodyguard" fell on top of me. He pulled me back up, shouting obscenities and kicking me ruthlessly. The passengers disembarked. I could hear the sound of an ambulance outside.

Two uniformed officers walked in. I didn't know where we were. Another officer walked into the first-class compartment where I was being held. He demanded that I be turned over. An Israeli officer declared, "She is our prisoner. Get out of here. This is Israeli property."

The first two men stood their ground. Then the Israeli pilot, yes, the pilot, in the presence of two British officers, came out of his cockpit, lifted me off my seat, and gave me a couple of vicious kicks in the bottom. The British officers screamed, "Shame," and pushed him aside. More British officers stepped into the fray, identifying themselves as members of Scotland Yard.

The captain told them, "To hell with you and your government. She is my prisoner. Get out of this plane." The British officers tried to seize me. Three Israelis pulled me in one direction by my trussed-up legs; the British pulled my hands in the other in a tug-of-war which the British won. A great husky English officer carried me over his shoulders and threw me down to the waiting arms of two other officers below.

I was in British hands. I knew it would be safer here for me than in Tel Aviv.

The British placed Patrick and me in some kind of police ambulance. I was hoping against hope that Patrick would live. In a few minutes, a nurse told an officer beside her something, but I didn't hear it. Then she took the oxygen mask off Patrick's mouth. I knew he was dead. I pleaded with the British to untie me. They did after they persuaded me to remain calm.

I stood beside Patrick's body. I held his hands; I surveyed his wounds; I touched his smashed head; I kissed his lips in a spirit of camaraderie and love. I wept unashamedly.

I spoke to him, "Patrick, now you have joined Che in revolutionary love. You are an inspiration for the weak and oppressed. The Palestinians shall build you monuments in their hearts and in their liberated homeland. I long for the hour of liberation under leaders of your stature and selfless dedication."

In less than twenty minutes, the ambulance arrived at Hillingdon Hospital. Patrick Arguello, age twenty-seven, father of three children, a Nicaraguan citizen of the world, born in San Francisco, USA, was pronounced dead. What had prompted someone halfway across the world from Palestine to undertake this dangerous mission?

Patrick was a revolutionary Communist. His gallant action was a gesture of international solidarity. A flame of life was extinguished; it lit the world for a moment; it blazed a trail on the road back to Palestine. Arguello lives, so do my people, so does the revolution!

At Hillingdon Hospital, I was given a general check-up and X-rayed. I was surrounded by a crush of people who seemed to have very little to do with my medical examination. The doctor pronounced me "fit to go," though neither he nor anyone else around me could have imagined how beat I was and how everything in me ached.

I was asked by someone who didn't look like a nurse who I was. I said, "I am a commando from the Popular Front for the Liberation of Palestine."

"This is not a name," a voice shouted.

"That's my name. I do not wish to talk further."

As people wandered around trying to extract confessions from me or statements, the familiar face of a journalist appeared in the crowd, but I couldn't place him. He must have recognized my voice immediately.

He said, "That's Leila."

A police officer said, "What Leila?"

"That's Leila Khaled, the girl who hijacked the TWA last year," the journalist replied.

"Are you sure?"

"Yes, I am."

The officer asked if Leila was my name. I smiled but refused to comment. I was taken to West Drayton police station where I spent the night. Here, the police tried to interrogate me. I absolutely refused to utter a single word beyond "I am a commando from the Popular Front," unless they agreed to recognize me as a commando and treat me as a war prisoner.

At West Drayton, the only unpleasant incident was when an immigration officer came in with a sheaf of papers, read me all sorts of legal instructions, and informed me that I was refused legal entry to Britain. I said, "Wonderful. Release me now." He said, "No," and wanted me to sign his ridiculous papers, acting as if I were some kind of British outlaw. I ordered him out.

The first two nights were a nightmare. I worried about what was taking place in Jordan and what had happened to the other planned hijackings. I felt terrible because I had failed to seize and retain the El-Al flight gig, and I felt shattered over the death of comrade Arguello. These two thoughts were constantly on my mind. I couldn't sleep for an hour without waking up, finding myself engaged in another make-believe battle. I was lonely and exhausted.

I said very little to the women who constantly accompanied me. The only relationship I had with them was "What time is it?"—a question posed as frequently as I could to ease my boredom. But one guard provoked me, "Why did you do it? It's a monstrous act," she said. I left without being able to explain to her why. However, she was kind to me and assisted me when the police moved me to Ealing. She put a blanket over my face and wished me well.

I was moved to Ealing police station on September 7. Here, I was placed in a cell by myself. Two women officers guarded me. At first, both seemed to resent me. We exchanged few words. I refused to eat. I only smoked and drank black coffee. I asked to see newspapers. They said I could read a women's magazine if I wanted. I said, "No thanks."

On September 8, I met Chief Superintendent Frew and Inspectors Bruce and Laidlaw.

I said to them, "I will talk if I am recognized as a commando." They agreed on the condition that I would tell the truth.

**Frew:** "What's your name?"

**Khaled:** "Leila Khaled."

**Frew:** "That's a lie."

**Khaled:** "Then, what is my name?"

**Frew:** "Khaled is an assumed name."

**Khaled:** "My assumed name is Shadiah Abu Ghazalah; she was one of our great fighters..."

Frew interrupted me, "Oh, please, please don't harangue us. Answer questions specifically." He showed me a pistol and asked me to identify it. I said it was one of several Israeli pistols brandished in my face. He showed me a pistol, which I later found out had been Patrick's, but since I hadn't seen it before, I said I didn't know to whom it belonged. He didn't believe me.

He then demanded, "How did you obtain those strange bodies?" referring to the hand grenades.

I answered him tersely: "They were given to me by the PF."

"Who issued this passport to you?"

"The PF," I said.

"Where were you going to take the plane?"

"Somewhere."

"Where?"

"Somewhere," I insisted.

"Who is Abd Arheem Jaber?" Now I brightened up and decided to deliver my first brief speech and refuse to talk further if I were stopped.

The officers sensed my determination and remained silent.

"Jaber is a Palestinian hero in Zionist dungeons. He is one of our underground commando leaders who struck terror in the heart of the enemy and throughout his cities. Before he was captured by the enemy on September 21, 1968, he fought courageously until his ammunition ran out. He held the enemy until most of his comrades managed to disappear in the face of American-made Sikorsky helicopters.

He lived among the peasants of Palestine, and he organized and trained them and spread revolutionary ideas. His most daring act was his challenge to General Sharif Nassir, uncle of King Hussein. Sharif Nassir was addressing a Jordanian platoon before the reactionary regime dispatched them to Yemen to help with the counter-revolutionary attempt to restore the deposed Imamate there.

Jaber stood up to Sharif Nassir and said, "Instead of sending us to Yemen to fight UAR troops and Yemeni radicals, why not send us to Tel Aviv to fight the real enemy of Palestine?"

Sharif Nassir, who is quick with the gun, found Jaber a bit quicker. Jaber was dishonorably discharged but upheld his dignity. I could tell you a lot more about the operations he masterminded in the occupied territories, but I want you to understand one thing: Jaber was held incommunicado for four months, and the enemy couldn't break his will in spite of the torture, physical and psychological, inflicted on him. I assure you I am of the same stuff. I trust you understand now why my unit was called the Abd Arahman Jaber Commando Unit.

The British officers listened stony-faced. When I had finished, Frew resumed his questioning.

"In this note written by you, Miss Khaled," Frew said, "it says Shadiah and her colleagues. Who are your colleagues?"

"What colleagues?" I asked. I paused briefly, then said, "It is quite possible that there were others on the plane whom I didn't know. Why, did you find someone else?" I inquired innocently.

"Miss Khaled," Frew said, "I have grey hair."

I promptly interrupted, "That's not from me. That's because you have a nagging wife."

Frew smiled to himself, "I think you are a very intelligent woman."

"I reject your compliments," I shot back as the verbal battle continued. I tried unsuccessfully to appear indignant and told the trio that as an Arab-Palestinian woman, I refused to accept compliments from fascist pigs who held me as a prisoner.

Frew shuffled through his collection of documents and retorted, "Why would an Arab-Palestinian woman try to blow up a plane on which there were Palestinian Arabs?"

I was not antagonized. "Oh," I said, "you have already decided that I am guilty of a crime that wasn't even committed before giving me the benefit of a British trial in court."

"All the witnesses said you tried to blow up the plane."

"Mr. Frew," I said, "they are a bunch of Zionist liars. Besides, why don't you hold a public inquiry and let every one of the witnesses be cross-examined?"

He cleverly interjected, "Do you think you're a coward, Miss Khaled?"

"Look," I replied, "I had orders to seize the plane, not to blow it up. I am no Kamikaze pilot. I care about people. If I wanted to blow up the plane, no one could have prevented me."

"Where did you board the plane? In Tel Aviv?" Frew inquired.

"I boarded it at Schiphol Airport in Amsterdam."

"How many other hijackings did you plan?"

"None."

"Two others have taken place," he informed me. Surprised and pleased, I tried not to show any reaction to his statement.

Then Frew said to me, "The Israelis have asked for your extradition. Would you like to be extradited to Israel?"

I didn't know the meaning of the word extradition and asked him to explain the implications. He did and added, "If you're extradited, the Israelis are likely to torture you."

"Well, Mr. Frew, then you know about Israel's torture chambers, brainwashing sessions, and physical shaming.

That's good. I am glad you know. I think others should too. Anyhow, if I am extradited, I will only be number twenty thousand and one. Just a statistic. I assure you, I won't break down under Zionist torture."

"I insist you're a very intelligent girl," Frew declared.

"I insist I do not accept your compliments. Give me a cigarette and a drink of water, please," I said humorously. In this relaxed atmosphere, I told the officers that I had committed no crime against the British and I could see no reason why I was being kept in a British jail. They said they didn't know either. I asked if any Israelis were also held in jail.

"None," they said.

I exploded: "Why not? Don't you know they executed my comrade in cold blood?"

"Your colleague was killed in battle. The coroner's verdict says his death was 'lawful homicide,'" Frew pointed out.

"Shame on the British courts," I cried out. "How could they make such a decision on the basis of biased evidence and without even interrogating me? It is the Star Chamber all over again. This time it is directed from Tel Aviv and Washington."

The atmosphere became tense as I gazed furiously at each officer. I muttered, "That's British justice," as they filed out. I was taken back to my cell. I had an intense headache that evening. The guards watched me closely as I marched back and forth restlessly.

On September 9, Mr. Frew visited me once again. He asked where I would like to go if extradited. I said to my homeland, Palestine. I demanded that I be released immediately and threatened dire consequences if the British continued my detention. That very day, a BOAC VC-10 was hijacked. I knew my release was imminent. Mr. Frew returned to tell me that evening that I must have known what was going on.

I said, "The Front knows what it is doing. I need not wait for a recommendation of clemency from a British jury."

On September 10, the ghost of Patrick haunted me. I couldn't stay my tears. I couldn't eat because Patrick had died hungry; I remembered that every day and tried to stop eating to pacify myself. The matron tried to calm me; she was a kindly woman and gave me helpful advice, but feelings of sadness and anguish aren't something that can be erased by a few motherly words. I was cheered up a little, however, when I learned that the PF was demanding my return in exchange for BOAC passengers.

Mr. Frew came in to inquire about Patrick's passport and asked, "Who was your partner, Leila?" He had closed the door behind him.

I said, "My name is not Leila, but Miss Leila Khaled, a commando from the Popular Front. Is that clear, Mr. Frew?" He was surprised that I was being so formal. I chuckled and tantalized him further: "According to your own rules, you have no right to be here in the absence of another female companion. By the way, when will I have the pleasure of facing British justice?" Frew was confused. He mumbled a few incoherent words and withdrew to reopen the door. He was somewhat apologetic as he asked if there was something he could do for me.

"Yes," I said, "I would like to knit sweaters for our commandos. Would you be kind enough to provide me with some wool and needles?" He promised to try but didn't think the rules would allow it. I requested a pencil and a piece of paper. He gave me a two-inch pencil. Though I felt drowsy and had a toothache, I penned my first note to Patrick.

Today is day four since we embarked on our immortal journey. Your spirit fills me with hope that the cause we embraced is just and honorable. You have given your life for a people you didn't know, for a people continents apart from your homeland, for a people who haven't seen your photograph.

Though I know you not, I know you more than any other man I encountered in my life or any other hero I read or dreamt about. I always longed to know people who love others more than themselves; I always admired men who sacrificed their lives for the cause of liberty; I always adored people who walked naked before the sun, not fearing its scorching rays, and said no to the enemies of light, life, and progress.

In dying for Palestine, you have become the symbol that lightens our oppression; you have also become the joyous burden that propels us onward to end that oppression. In joining our struggle for dignity and peoplehood, you have given us a lesson in international solidarity and brotherhood and cemented the bond of affection between the people of Latin America and the people of Palestine.

You wrote history by shedding your blood for others; you united continents by your all-encompassing spirit; you ascended to the realm of Olympian gods by your life-inspiring commitment. You are at once a Lafayette, a Byron, a Norman Bethune, a Che Guevara—a Patrick Arguello, a martyr for Palestinian freedom. You are not dead. You live. You will live forever! You are the patron saint of Palestine.

In revolution,
Leila.

---

September 11 was a day for banter. It started with a visit from the envoy of Honduras, a corpulent, mustached feudal lord. Mr. Frew introduced him as his excellency, the Consul of Honduras.

He asked, "How did you obtain this Honduran passport?"

I answered contemptuously: "Did the Popular Front disguise you and send you here as a fictitious banana republic ambassador?" His excellency was infuriated. He departed like a vanquished Napoleon. What a sad state of affairs for officialdom, for a Latin consul to be ridiculed and insulted by a Palestinian or a nobody hijacker. How humiliating!

Mr. Frew was appalled but not surprised by my reaction. I blamed him for failing to fulfill his promise of knitting material. He apologized and explained.

"You are not allowed to have sharp instruments in your possession." He wanted to know if the Front would explode the plane with the passengers, as was reported by the "objective" British press that day.

"Yes," I said unhesitatingly.

"What?" he asked. "Have you no humanity?"

"Humanity, my foot!" I shouted. "You should be ashamed to utter such a word in the West. If you have any integrity, you'd remove that word from your dictionaries and declare it a non-English word." I started making a speech on Zionism and imperialism and how the British vampired the Arab world, but Mr. Frew deflated me this time.

He interrupted, "Miss Leila Khaled, perhaps our government is imperialist. Please stop your speech-making." I felt undercut and later asked my "bodyguards" why Mr. Frew didn't defend the government. They explained that there were many members of the Labour Party at Ealing who were not necessarily sympathetic to the Conservative government.

On September 12, I tried to take a different tack after hearing that the imperialist planes had been blown up. Since all kinds of strikes were going on in Britain, I thought my "bodyguards" should go on strike in sympathy with their fellow workers. I suggested that since they were "my prisoners," they should stage a revolt and join their fellow workers on strike. As I was urging them to rebel, Mr. Frew walked in.

He took a deep breath and said, "What are you up to now?"

"Mr. Frew," I said, "these prisoners deserve to be free."

"What prisoners?" he enquired. "Those poor masses working night and day here."

"O.K. You win this time," he said paternally.

As Mr. Frew sat checking his files, I decided to badger him. "I know the Home Office is violating British justice, habeas corpus, and other concepts of justice, but does the Ealing Hilton have to violate the laws of hygiene too, Mr. Frew?"

He scratched his head and enquired further. I informed him that I hadn't had a bath in six days. He quickly arranged for me to be marched to the fifth floor, accompanied by four police matrons who insisted on having me undress in their presence as each guarded a corner of the narrow shower room.

September 13 was a bad day for me. I felt ill most of the day and couldn't sleep that night. The doctor was called in. He pleaded with me to eat more than just a cheese sandwich and coffee and gave me two sleeping tablets. They had a terrible effect on me. That night was a nightmare for everybody except me. They thought I was about to die, but I surprised them and woke up feeling as if my head weighed a ton. When I opened my eyes at five-thirty a.m., everyone was practically in tears. That charming little matron was truly relieved and delighted to see me revive. It was apparent that she had had a sleepless night, as had most people around me.

The next two weeks I settled into an established routine. There were no further interrogations. I was allowed to use the matron's rooms and to roam within a ten-yard radius without being followed.

Political issues in Jordan, especially after the seventeenth, preoccupied me and became the focal point of my discussions with Frew and others. I was given a bundle of letters that had arrived at Ealing: some denounced me; others supported the cause; one contained a marriage proposal. I was not permitted to answer any of them, but I was permitted to write to my parents and some close friends. I volunteered to translate the contents, but Mr. Frew told me that Her Majesty's Government had its own interpreters.

It didn't surprise me that a full-scale massacre was underway in Jordan. Isolated in a British cage, however, I did not appreciate the magnitude and extent of Hussein's terror. It seemed, judging from reports in the British press, that the incident was a continuation of the policy of harassment, intimidation, and terror instituted in November of 1968 and continued sporadically since then.

Although it was obvious that the latest combat engulfed the whole country, it was not so obvious as the final liquidation attempt on the part of the monarchy.

Many have alleged, without justification, that the PFLP precipitated the massacres by the Jordanian regime of

September 1970 with the multiple "hijackings" we undertook. Such a simple explanation.

The well-conceived plot by the Jordanian authorities to eliminate the Palestinian revolution cannot be accepted. The massacre of September and the subsequent mopping-up operations, which took place while the Arab states fulminated, should convince everyone that the Arab kings and colonels regarded the Palestinian resistance as a dangerous movement threatening their regimes and potentially engulfing the region in an international civil war of the working class versus the forces of oppression.

During those momentous months, it became clear that Hussein was prepared to invite Israel to take over "his kingdom" rather than allow the resistance to topple him. America almost intervened to "rescue" its citizens and maintain Hussein in power. The components in this drama included a power-hungry Hashemite ruling clique, prepared to commit any treachery to keep the reins of power; general Arab silence, which can only be interpreted as acquiescence to the massacre; and the American Zionist conspiracy hatched between Golda Meir and Nixon in Washington.

On September 17, the British guards, whether on their own initiative or under instructions from their superiors, urged me to ask for political asylum. To me, it was a repugnant form of abdication, and I rejected the idea immediately. In fact, I demanded to be released so I could join my comrades in Jordan. The British bided their time and negotiated as partners of the so-called "Berne Five," under pressure from the Americans and the Israelis.

I am certain the Germans, the Swiss, and the British would have exchanged hostages for our prisoners had it not been for Zionist and American insistence on a unified front—an action which showed how little the Europeans cared for their own citizens compared to those of Zionist Israel and the American behemoth. Their justification for such callous deeds was that they were upholding international law and morality and defending "innocent passengers," but let's not deceive ourselves; the interests of Dick Nixon and Golda Meir were placed ahead of those of Britain, Germany, and "neutral" Switzerland.

The turmoil in Jordan disturbed me deeply. I tried to maintain my composure and act naturally, but it was a difficult job. Mr. Frew was a daily visitor. He wondered why Muslims fought each other instead of the enemy. I lectured him on the nature of class society and explained that the good little British-manufactured King of Jordan was part of the enemy camp. Frew listened intently, but like most of his Western compatriots, he was unable to grasp the idea of social class and its historic implications. He only accused me of being bitter. I said I was more than bitter; I was full of class hatred and aspired for nothing less than the complete obliteration of the Jordanian monarchy and retinue. Frew's prescription for the remedy of my class consciousness was a week's stay in "democratic" Britain after my release.

I said, "I'll be happy to stay in Britain until Christmas if I am released immediately so as to enjoy the fruits of British democracy."

Frew detected my sarcastic tone. "Now," he said, "I wish you would go back to Jordan before I lose my wife."

"Tell your wife not to worry, Mr. Frew. I have no intention of marrying a fatherly British cop. If I do marry, it will be an Arab revolutionary or a simple peasant, not a British lord, not a Greek shipping magnate, not an American industrial baron. Is that clear, Mr. Frew?"

I followed the Jordanian civil war in the British press. When I began reading reports about the "Syrian intervention," I deduced from fragmented editorial comments that an Israeli-US invasion was being contemplated. When, however, it was reported that the "Syrian column" had been defeated by "brave" Jordanians and forced to withdraw, I realized that the regime was not on the verge of dethronement. But when I saw Hussein and Arafat shake hands in the presence of kings and presidents, I knew the revolution was betrayed.

At that moment, I am sure I could have unhesitatingly gunned down every participant in that conference. I could no longer withhold my fury; I could see the writing on the wall: the resistance was dead as a historic force. I truly cried for the blood of martyrs in Jordan, the blood bartered away at the Cairo Hilton, the Kubbe Palace, and the Arab League.

Headquarters. I could not forgive the Arab League for the blood of Patrick, whose body still lay in a British morgue while counterrevolutionary "peace" was signed. I knew the fighters would repudiate the leadership and, in time, form their own revolutionary vanguard party.

I knew it had to be done; I knew the Front was going to do it. In the ensuing months, however, Arafat and Co. still refused to understand that the Palestinian Arab revolution was in fundamental contradiction to the Arab decadent social orders. Hussein crushed the resistance physically in Jordan and drove the guerrillas out in July 1971, and the "resistance leaders," with the exception of the Popular Front and a few independents, accepted Saudi-Egyptian mediation and were still prepared to negotiate with Jordan and embrace Hussein and Hassan.

Early on September 28, it was reported that President Nasser was dying. The news didn't strike me as real, nor did I fathom the implication of his impending death. I was still too frenzied over the Arafat-Hussein accord to think clearly.

Late in the day, however, it was reported that President Nasser had died. I was stunned, emotionally paralyzed. The feelings I had when Che and Ho died returned. This time perhaps more poignantly, for I was, as every Arab was at one time or another, an admirer of Nasser. He was one of the greatest Arab leaders of the modern era. As a giant among dwarfs, he symbolized everything noble, great, and weak among the Arabs.

He was from us and one of us; he was a leader of men. I felt a part of me died with him. I was happy I had lived in the age of Nasser. I will only be happier to live in a liberated Palestine.

Mr. Frew and those around me saw how sad I was. They couldn't understand why I should be so distressed over the death of someone I had denounced the day before. They couldn't understand that Nasser was the first champion of anti-imperialism in my world.

On September 29, Frew intimated that I might soon be released. I checked the newspapers closely for clues as to when the last six hostages were going to be surrendered to the International Red Cross Committee. They finally were on the thirtieth of September, 1970. The moment the hostages reached Cyprus, I was instructed to prepare for departure. There was no indication of my destination.

I bade my British friends farewell, kisses and all, and promised to send more customers to the Ealing Hilton, where clients have bodyguards and accommodation is free.

At six-thirty, Mr. Frew came and asked me to which country I would like to go. I said confidently, "The decision has already been taken by my commanders. By the way, where am I being taken?" Frew didn't answer, and no one answered the question in the next few hours. I was told that since I was a soldier, I was expected to abide by the rules as I was being moved out of Britain. I agreed and followed orders to the letter.

The matrons told me that people were lining up in the streets to see me, but they were going to be sadly disappointed as I would be taken out lying, covered up in a van. I was surprised to be accompanied by a whole convoy of police cars and motorcycles. I was allowed one quick look at the crowd assembled around Ealing police station before being taken to a military airport.

As I boarded the helicopter, I flashed a victory sign to the photographers. I said goodbye to Mr. Frew and promised to visit the "Ealing" again. "No," he cried out, "come to Britain, not to the 'Ealing.'"

We traveled by helicopter for about an hour and then landed at another nameless airport. I noted to the captain that helicopters are more difficult to hijack than regular planes. He didn't appreciate my sense of humor. Then we boarded a Comet for an unannounced destination. I still couldn't find out where I was going.

Then I heard a member of the crew saying, "there is another woman to come." I knew instantly it had to be Amina Dhahbour, who was being held by the Swiss in Zurich. Suddenly we descended in Munich. The airport was a garrison. From my window, I counted the armored cars. I was ordered to take the last seat on the plane.

Three brothers from the Action Organisation, Mufid Abdul Rahman, Hanabi, and Nashaat, were brought aboard. I knew none of them, and we were not allowed to shake hands.

The next stop was Zurich, where my inspiration, Amina, and comrades Ibrahim Tewfiq and Mohammad Abu Al-Haifa came aboard. I wanted at least to hug Amina, but it was not permitted. We just greeted each other from afar. Each of the passengers had his own bodyguard. None was handcuffed.

The night of September 30 was a long one. The journey to Cairo was the longest I ever endured. I slept periodically. We had to remain seated at all times.

We arrived in Cairo on October 1, 1970, at eight a.m. The city was in mourning for the death of President Nasser. The British, German, and Swiss consuls met us at the airport. Each one of us was dutifully taken in hand by "his" consul and turned over to the Egyptian authorities. Protocol reigned.

I was astonished to find out that Patrick's body wasn't with us, but there were no British around to denounce or Arab leaders to threaten. We were taken to an Egyptian "guesthouse" and held there for eleven days. We were told that we were being held there for "security reasons."

On October 12, we were flown to Damascus, and each commando rejoined his or her unit. Before returning to Beirut, however, I visited my friend Colonel Ali Zaza, the man who had accused me of working for Egyptian intelligence in the TWA affair.

"Colonel," I said, as I barged into his office, "I trust you are convinced now that the Popular Front and I are nobody's tools."

"I am," he said.

"Wouldn't you like to keep me in your guesthouse again?"

"No, Leila, this time you can be my guest for lunch."

"No thank you, Colonel," I said. "I have to report back to my unit in Beirut within two hours. See you on the battlefield in Palestine!"

I went to Beirut in mid-October and held a press conference at Al-Hadaf's office, pointing out that Patrick was murdered by the Israelis and that the British excused the crime that took place in their airspace. To this date, the British have refused to put their "evidence" before a competent authority for inspection, and the autopsy report remains confidential.

For the next few weeks, I spent most of my time giving press interviews and preparing to marry a fellow fighter, Bassim, an Iraqi Arab revolutionary. We got married on November 26, 1970, spent a week together, and then returned to our separate tasks.

# PART THREE:
## Conclusion

8 The Fascist Tide and the Arab Revolution

---

Against me, he is a lion; against the enemy, he is an ostrich. The Jordanian soldiers carry themselves like lions when it is a question of the unarmed Palestinian refugees, but when the time came, they did not know how to die in defense of Jerusalem. — President Houari Boumedienne of the Republic of Algeria

## The Supreme Objective of the Palestine Liberation Movement

The total liberation of Palestine, the dismantlement of the Zionist state apparatus, and the construction of a socialist society in which both Arabs and Jews can live in peace and harmony are our goals. To achieve our objective, we have adopted the strategy of people's war and protracted armed struggle. We have no other alternative; we see no other possible option to dislodge the Zionists from Palestine.

Our struggle will be long and arduous because the enemy is powerful, well-organized, and well sustained from abroad. We shall win because we represent the wave of the future, because we are the immense majority of the oppressed, because mankind is on our side, and above all because we are determined to achieve victory.

**The Goal of the Arab States**

The goal of the Arab states is "the elimination of the consequences of aggression" or the restoration of the status quo ante, not the liberation of the whole of Palestine. The Arab states contend that they can force Israel to withdraw to the June 4, 1967, borders by a judicious combination of diplomacy and conventional warfare, not by armed struggle and revolutionary ideology.

They stress the "political solution" and accept mediation by the UN and the major powers as a fait accompli. They try to persuade their American and Soviet friends to pressure Israel to withdraw. They also periodically engage in spasmodic military actions to demonstrate their determination to regain the occupied territories.

Israel still holds every inch of territory it conquered in 1967, and in all likelihood, it will continue to do so, barring profound changes in Arab and American policies. To secure the home front, the Arab governments have strengthened and modernized their intelligence services; both "progressives" and "conservatives" are collaborating effectively to stem the tide of revolution at home.

The aim of America is "regional stability" under its ascendant power. In this age of neocolonialism, America has its storming gendarme in Israel and its militia in the reactionary and military cliques of the Arab world. If its calculations go awry, however, America wouldn't find it difficult to intervene directly to protect its "citizens and interests" or to help a local potentate ward off the "menace of communism."

America is firmly entrenched in the world of black gold; it has no intention of ever sacrificing the flow of bullion into its banks. Indeed, it is prepared to risk nuclear war to keep us "free" and "safe for democracy." America doesn't love the naked fakirs of the Arab world, nor does it care for every little forgotten Jew the world over. America cares for America, and America is Wall Street, the Pentagon, their agents and manipulators in the government bureaucracy, and the hordes of priests, journalists, and professors which populate the churches, the media, and the universities.

The aim of the Soviet Union is the neutralization of the US and its eventual expulsion from the Middle East. As an advocate of co-existence, the peaceful transition to socialism, and the non-capitalist road to development, the USSR supports the "Arab national regimes" in their anti-imperialist struggle, provides them with loans for industrial projects, and weapons to fight the Israeli conquerors. As a sponsor of the "political solution," the Soviet Union recognizes the legitimacy of Israel, respects its sovereignty and the territorial integrity of states, and demands the "impartial" implementation of UN resolutions.

The Soviet Union is a champion of "peace and co-existence," not of people's war and revolutionary violence. With the "progressive" Arab regimes, the Soviet Government stands for the domestication, not the elimination, of the resistance and the Arab revolution. America, Israel, and Arab reactionaries stand on the other hand for the liquidation of the resistance and the obliteration of the Arab revolution.

The overriding objective of Israel is the peace of the bayonet: the "peace" of conquest, the dictated and imposed "peace" of the "defensive" forces of Dayan, and the "peace" of North American and West European rabbis and their congregations.

In brief, the peace of America, Israel, and Zionism is the peace of total destruction of the Palestinian people, the domination of neighboring states, and the perpetuation of Zionist supremacy in the Middle East. Since Israel cannot rely forever on the generosity of world Jewry, the blank cheque at the Export-Import Bank of America, or expect a new kind of German reparations, it needs new guarantees to achieve and maintain a self-sustaining and viable economy. It needs a continuing influx of immigrants and dollars, and it needs a "peace with tension" to obtain the support and concern of friend and ally.

Therefore, Israel favors the present conditions of unchallenged dominance in the absence of a more durable, "contractual peace." However, Israel would be prepared to sign a "peace treaty," forgo the possibility of further territorial conquest, and withdraw to the June 4 borders, with the exception of Jerusalem, under two conditions:

1. Access to Arab markets
2. Ownership of the oil and mineral resources of the Gulf of Suez

Nothing less will induce Israel to withdraw or make serious territorial concessions other than total defeat or American decisive pressure. The latter two possibilities are out of the question because the Arab armies are incapable of waging the kind of war required, and if they were, both the Soviet Union and the US would not permit them to undertake it.

Secondly, the US has not exerted enough pressure to force Israel to withdraw. Indeed, if anything, the US has implicitly endorsed the territorial conquests of Zionism by the continuous "sale" of Phantoms and Skyhawks, and the outflow of millions of American tax-free dollars. Thus, the state of "neither war nor peace" will continue into the foreseeable future, whatever ad hoc settlement may be attained under UN or great power auspices.

In spite of the apparent differences among the US, the Soviet Union, the Arab states, and Israel, a convergence of interests in the spring and summer of 1970 enabled them to coalesce either overtly or covertly. The implicit accord they reached manifested itself in what was termed the Rogers Peace Proposals—proposals which entailed a cease-fire agreement between the Arab states and Israel and acceptance of the UN resolutions concerning "peace and security" in the Middle East.

The full significance of the accord was revealed in September of 1970 when King Hussein proceeded to eliminate the resistance in southern Jordan as his part of the agreement in Rogers' peace. In mid-August, Hussein's target was Irbid, a city in the north where "refugee" and resistance camps were mercilessly attacked, people killed, and bodies mutilated. The talk of forthcoming Armageddon was in the air; everything foreboded ill for the resistance unless it seized the initiative and decided to settle who ruled in Jordan.

Skirmishing continued in Amman, Jerush, Zerga, and Irbid. Hussein was in hot pursuit of the resistance: daily he tested its will to fight. The resistance was preoccupied with its own pre-eminence and power; it expressed its fearlessness in bombastic declarations but agreed upon no contingency plans. Very few anticipated the massive barbarity and bestiality of Hussein and Co. Indeed, the resistance leadership thought it would muddle through the gathering storm and perhaps emerge unscathed and possibly even strengthened by Hussein's direct assault. Fateh's right-wing leadership and other sectors of the movement could not conceive that Hussein was out to decapitate and annihilate the resistance.

During this period of internal dismay, disarray, and disintegration, I was on my way to Europe to carry out a minor aspect of the Front's offensive strategy to topple Hussein. But he and his CIA advisers preempted us on September 1, 1970. He put his well-established and well-known plan into effect: he disclosed an assassination plot and attributed it to the Popular Front, hoping to split the ranks of the resistance and pit the fighters against each other. The Western and Arab press dutifully reported Hussein's charges and distinguished between "honest" revolutionaries who wanted to fight.

Israel and "terrorists" were trying to precipitate a civil war in Jordan. The plot unfolded rapidly as Hussein scornfully told Iraq not to meddle in Jordanian internal affairs and appealed to the great powers, including the Soviet Union, to restrain the "hotheads," all the while drawing their attention to Iraq's threatened intervention if Hussein did not stop firing on the guerrillas.

The Arab League Council was called into an emergency session, appealing for an immediate cessation of hostilities (September 5 and 6) and reactivating the four-nation committee, established as a result of the June fighting, to oversee the implementation of the July 10 accord between Hussein and the resistance.

Meanwhile, the Palestine National Congress failed to come to grips with the issue; it merely conducted another session of poetic oratory with no binding decisions. The resistance was hemmed in; the leadership still refused to act in concert. Then came the epoch-making strategy of the Popular Front; all the enemies of the revolution were outflanked on September 6, 1970.

Hussein's authority was immediately shattered; Israel's European and American allies were put on the defensive; the Palestinian and Arab people rejoiced and applauded our deed; the world stood shocked and forced to take heed of Palestine. Palestine was on the lips of everyone the world over for a week. Our Six Day War began: for the first time in modern history, the Palestinians were on the center stage and we were directing the play. We tasted the meaning of sovereignty; we reaped the fruit of the summer harvest; we gloried in the joy of nationhood; we became a people for a whole week.

But nobody congratulated us openly. All condemned us "universally." But we were oblivious to the reactions of an insensitive world whose tender conscience did not have room for the Palestinians—a world that had built a shrine to Zion and couldn't afford a plaque for Palestine.

Our Zionist prosecutors had a niche in the Western pantheon; we were a past memory for archaeologists to explore; the world sat in judgment on a subject it recognized as a "refugee"; the refugee said no to charity, no to pity, no to benevolent despotism—but YES to Palestine, to liberation, to revolution! The seizure of British, Swiss, and American planes turned things topsy-turvy for the enemy.

It was no longer able to dictate "peace" terms.

What is startling, however, is that the Western proponents of "humanity and peace" resorted to the threat and use of violence in order to safeguard their "sovereign rights." They initially pressured Hussein into carrying out their will, which he did in an 11-day war of annihilation against the resistance.

Here is the testimony of Arnaud de Borchgrave of Newsweek (October 5, 1970, p. 38):

"In almost a quarter of a century of foreign reporting, I cannot recall anything remotely similar to what I have seen in Jordan. I have witnessed intertribal massacres in Africa and the slow, steady bloodletting in Vietnam. But there has been nothing like the urban devastation—both of life and property—that Amman has suffered."

When Hussein appeared to be failing at the beginning of the onslaught, he, along with his Israeli and American allies, concocted the Syrian intervention myth in order to facilitate the planned intervention of both America and Israel in Jordan. The evidence for the myth, of course, was the Palestine Liberation Army's forward thrust from

Syria (September 20), which almost annihilated the Fortieth Brigade, Hussein's pride.

Admittedly, Syria did not hamper the PLA effort, and it probably approved of it and supported it. But the PLA's foray into Jordan provided the US and Israel with the pretext to threaten intervention of their own unless "Syrian forces withdrew."

The whole plot must have been well thought out when Golda Meir arrived "unexpectedly" in Washington on the seventeenth, the same day that Hussein planned to pulverize the resistance. Mrs. Meir was closeted with Nixon, and both "amicably" agreed to continue their discussions in the light of developments in Jordan.

On September 18, the Chicago Sun-Times reported on a long "private" meeting its editorial board had with Nixon the night before: the report said that America was prepared to intervene directly "should Syria and Iraq enter the conflict and tip the military balance against the government forces loyal to King Hussein."

The cat was out of the bag two days before the alleged Syrian intervention was supposed to have taken place. Meir and Nixon decided to intervene. Therefore, to give credence to the myth of Syrian intervention, Secretary of State William Rogers pointedly asked the Soviet Union (September 20) to urge Syria to pull back and issued a statement which read in part:

"We've been informed that tank forces have invaded Jordan from Syria during the night and have moved toward Ramtha. We have also been informed that Jordanian armor is resisting this invasion.

We condemn this irresponsible and imprudent intervention of Syria into Jordan. This action carries with it the danger of broadened conflict. We call upon the Syrian government to end immediately this intervention in Jordan, and we urge all other concerned governments to impress upon the government of Syria the necessity of withdrawing the forces which have invaded Jordan."

Rogers, the underrated and soft-spoken arch-imperialist, was of the opinion that Syria had no right to intervene in Jordan, but that he and Abba Eban had a right to do so at the request of the established authority of King Hussein. Anyhow, whatever Mr. Rogers had to say was merely the tip of the iceberg of America's planned Operation Brass Strike, which was intended to restore Hussein to his throne had he fallen or had he been on the verge of falling.

According to the Times-Post news service (September 29), the 82nd Airborne Division began moving into full alert at Fort Bragg on September 20.

On orders from President Nixon, the signal directed the 14,000 paratroopers here to get ready for possible use in Jordan. Their mission: if so ordered, to descend on Amman and rescue 54 air-hijacked hostages, including 38 Americans, and some 400 other Americans living in the guerrilla-besieged Jordanian capital. Simultaneously alerted were about 2,000 troops in U.S. Army units in West Germany, ships of the Sixth Fleet in the Mediterranean, and 1,500 U.S. Marines aboard assault ships headed for the embattled area.

The implication was that, while the 82nd would concentrate on a lightning-quick, in-and-out rescue, the others might be sent in if King Hussein's army could not hold off the Palestinian guerrillas and Syrian and Iraqi forces supporting them.

In America's "open" society and "free" press, the Times-Post dispatch summarized the plans thus:

The 200-plus-man initial ready force could go to an intermediate stop for refueling—maybe the Azores, Spain, West Germany, or some other reasonable site—and then swoop down aboard their 500-mile-per-hour, 5,000-mile range G141s on Amman's International airport. If possible, they could land the planes. If the airport was insecure, the force could parachute down, equipment and all, and capture the field.

With the field secure and more increments arriving—not only men and guns but helicopters carried inside big transports—the assault force could be ready to move out within hours. Helicopters could be prepared for flight. Then they could attack specified areas, where the people to be rescued were, and, in the classic Vietnam tactic, hold off attackers with their heavy firepower while disgorging men who would then fan out to build a perimeter defense. Amman's few open spaces, like parks, were marked off as landing zones.

For such "intelligent" and "heroic" deeds, America was relying on Israeli intelligence, the speed and firepower of its armory, and the "love" of the Jordanian people for Richard Nixon, Spiro Agnew, Moshe Dayan, and Golda Meir. Moreover, America's planned action to maintain Hussein in power was disclosed by the New York Times

(October 8, 1970) on page one, in a story that also implicated the Soviet Union and the Arab States.

Here is a summary report of that long in-depth article:

**WASHINGTON—The United States and Israel were preparing to take coordinated military action in the recent Jordanian crisis, according to US and Israeli sources.**

This plan envisioned an Israeli attack on the Syrian tank forces that had entered Jordan if it appeared that King Hussein's army was incapable of stopping them. In this event, the United States would have used the Sixth Fleet and other units to safeguard Israel's rear and flanks from Egyptian or Soviet attacks from the Suez Canal area.

The plan was not put into effect because the Syrian tanks, harassed by King Hussein's jets and armor, began retreating into Syria. Informed sources here believe that it was the combination of Israel's troop buildup plus the US military alert—both well publicized—that sobered the Syrians and the Soviet Union.

President Nixon assumed personal direction of the intense diplomatic and military activity as the crisis approached its climax.

The bond between the US and Israel in this crisis was their joint determination that King Hussein must not be overthrown by outside intervention because they assumed he would be replaced by a regime closely linked to Moscow.

An urgent message from King Hussein asking the United States and Britain to consider what military support they could provide him gave impetus to the planning. But perhaps an equally strong force for quick action was the feeling in Washington that Israel would consider itself compelled to strike the Syrian forces if they continued to penetrate into Jordan in support of the guerrillas who were challenging King Hussein's authority. Another more publicized factor was concern about 400 US citizens and 54 hostages, including 38 Americans, in the hands of Palestinian guerrillas in Jordan at the time.

And, as if Hussein had not been sufficiently exposed as an imperialist-Zionist agent, Time Magazine came out with a full-page account (November 23, 1970, p. 34) describing his relations with Israel since 1968 and reporting that the tenth meeting had just been held in the Arava wilderness north of Elat between Hussein and Yigal Allon, Israel's Deputy Prime Minister.

In an atmosphere of amiability, Hussein, according to Time, informed Allon in a ninety-minute dialogue that his throne was secure, but the time was not ripe for unilateral discussions. The Time report concerning the crux of the matter and its interpretative comment was as follows:

Even so, one result of the border meeting is that broader negotiations with representatives of other Arab states can be expected to follow. Turning to the question of the guerrillas, the two leaders agreed that the fedayeen were a nuisance to both countries and that coordination was necessary to neutralize them. The King received promises of Israeli help.

Hussein and Allon also agreed to expand economic relations. At the same time, however, Hussein protested that Mrs. Meir was undercutting him by observing during her latest US visit that Palestinian statehood was only a question of re-drawing Jordan's boundaries. The King was prepared to grant Palestinian autonomy of a sort, he said, but under his rule, and not as the nucleus of an independent Palestinian state.

The civil war in Jordan was not an incidental phenomenon. It was part of America's global strategy to reverse the tide of history and to eliminate liberation movements everywhere. It was part of a war of reaction and suppression whose victims have been, in the main, the leaders and movements of the Third World since the Second World War.

Since most resistance movements have either been defeated, undermined, or contained, with the exception of the Vietnamese nationalists, it was imperative that the voices of revolution be stilled, or at least weakened in Palestine. Thus came the June War of 1967 that was intended as the grand finale in America's attempt to restore "sanity and order" in the world and rid mankind of the contagious virus of liberty and revolution.

The attempt failed temporarily, but in 1970-71 the Fascist tide once again flooded the Arab world: the consequences are not difficult to discern and evaluate.

The immediate victim in the all-encompassing war of Fascism was the resistance whose power, prestige, and effectiveness were eroded by the retreat of Fateh's right-wing leadership; they walked sheepishly to Hussein's slaughterhouse with the connivance of Arab regimes.

When the final assault came in July 1971, another fruitless Arab summit meeting was convened. Hussein imprisoned 2,300 guerrillas and drove the rest of the movement completely out of the Ajloun-Jerash area. No strongholds were left for the movement; its former headquarters offices were in ruins in Amman and elsewhere in Jordan.

Phase one of the revolution – revolutionism without ideology – was dead.

As America extended its influence and spread its wings of annihilation anew in the Middle East, the comrades-in-arms of President Nasser—"the Soviet wing" of Ali Sabri and Sami Sharaf—were charged with high treason (May 13, 1971) and removed from their strategic positions in the Egyptian state apparatus and the Arab Socialist Union.

President Sadat and his "brilliant" mentor, Mohammad Hassanein Heikal, moved closer to Washington and slowly detached themselves from the Soviet Union. This was done to redress the balance in favor of "non-alignment" and to reintegrate the middle classes into Egyptian society, improving its relations with the West. The cease-fire continued, and no actions on the Suez front took place as the re-Egyptianisation of Arab Egypt commenced in earnest in the aftermath of the upheaval.

In less than two months after the Egyptian bombshell, Hussein intensified his incessant attacks on the guerrillas. To the eternal shame of the Arab world, about one hundred Palestinian guerrillas took refuge in occupied Palestine and placed their fates in the hands of Dayan rather than die at the hands of King Hussein. The King proudly stated on July 18:

"We had no choice but to act against the commandos because they became a nuisance to many people and to the armed forces. The fighting is finished. This is final. Now there is no problem, and attempts are being made to bring them together and achieve a better solution. If need be, we are all fedayeen against the Israelis."

Asked if there were any new agreements with the guerrillas, Hussein stated, "The time has gone when the commandos could act according to their whim. The time has come for the state to determine the areas where they must stay. They must also respond to the state's instructions."

In other words, Hussein wanted a guerrilla movement to serve his and America's private interests, to help him recover "his" lost territory, and keep the Palestinians in check.

While Hussein's treachery was going on, a spark of hope appeared in the skies of the Arab homeland. In July 1971, the Hashem Attah movement seized power in Sudan and proclaimed the first Arab Workers' Republic. By July 22, Sadat and Qaddafi had bared their teeth and "heroically" abolished the republic. They restored Numeiry to power and instigated a communist witch-hunt throughout the Arab world.

To camouflage their deeds and create a diversion for the masses, Sadat, Qaddafi, and Assad formed the Federation of Arab Republics on September 1, allegedly as a first step to "Arab unity," but in fact, as a means of safeguarding their regimes from revolution.

Thus, the present Arab ruling cliques returned to the positions held by their predecessors on the eve of 1948: Islamic fundamentalism, class collaboration, and anti-communism. It would seem that the Arab ruling classes would rather embrace Zionism, live under the yoke of American imperialism, and retard the historic evolution of their societies than submit to the will of the masses, abdicate power, or let other forces of progress lead the revolution.

The petit bourgeoisie of the Arab world has become a spent historic force; it is incapable of coping with such crucial issues as oil, Israel, and poverty. Its approach was revealed in Sadat's speech on July 23, 1971, the nineteenth anniversary of the Egyptian revolution. He singled out the Popular Front for attack and contempt, declared war on Israel five times, withdrew twenty-five times, and applauded King Feisal for his moderation and statesmanship. No reference was made to the abolition of poverty, the struggle against imperialism, or the liberation of Palestine. Sadat's historic speech made it clear that the principal contradiction was not imperialism, but the revolution. He therefore formed a new axis with Feisal and decided to become the new arbiter of Palestinian and Arab fortunes.

Both are now trying to arrange for a rapprochement between the "honest" resistance groups and Hussein, and they have persuaded the Executive Committee of the PLO to go along, with the exception of the Popular Front. In September-October 1971, the resistance negotiated with Hussein in Jedda under Feisal's auspices.

The Popular Front, in conformity with the will of the fighters, disclosed that the Executive Committee had agreed to conciliation (September 8, 1971) and denounced the so-called mediation attempts of the personal representative of Feisal and Sadat.

With this exposure ends the story of Arabs in action and reaction with regard to twenty-three years of Palestinian Diaspora. But there is a ray of hope on the horizon: the people no longer believe their leaders, the underground forces are multiplying in number, and the Popular Front is deepening its roots—it is still the hope for the future of the Palestinian people.

Leila Khaled, 1971

Leila Khaled, 2002

Since this book was completed, Leila Khaled has been doing "mass political work," organizing the guerrilla camps and contriving to recruit supporters. She and I work closely together in the Popular Front for the Liberation of Palestine.

Now that Leila is known throughout the world, her picture having appeared in every western newspaper, we are not likely to permit her in the foreseeable future to participate in foreign, political, or military missions. Her role is now to work inside the Arab world for the day when our people can once again return to their homeland.

George Hajjar

February 1973

www.ingramcontent.com/pod-product-compliance
Lightning Source LLC
LaVergne TN
LVHW012053070526
838201LV00083B/4243